Devil's Advocates

DEVIL'S ADVOCATES is a series of books devoted to exploring the classics of horror cinema. Contributors to the series come from the fields of teaching, academia, journalism and fiction, but all have one thing in common: a passion for the horror film and a desire to share it with the widest possible audience.

'The admirable Devil's Advocates series is not only essential – and fun – reading for the serious horror fan but should be set texts on any genre course.'
Dr Ian Hunter, Reader in Film Studies, De Montfort University, Leicester

'Auteur Publishing's new Devil's Advocates critiques on individual titles... offer bracingly fresh perspectives from passionate writers. The series will perfectly complement the BFI archive volumes.' **Christopher Fowler,** *Independent on Sunday*

'Devil's Advocates has proven itself more than capable of producing impassioned, intelligent analyses of genre cinema... quickly becoming the go-to guys for intelligent, easily digestible film criticism.' *Horror Talk.com*

'Auteur Publishing continue the good work of giving serious critical attention to significant horror films.' ***Black Static***

 DevilsAdvocatesbooks

 DevilsAdBooks

Also available in this series

A Girl Walks Home Alone at Night Farshid Kazemi
Black Sunday Martyn Conterio
The Blair Witch Project Peter Turner
Blood and Black Lace Roberto Curti
The Blood on Satan's Claw David Evans-Powell
Candyman Jon Towlson
Cannibal Holocaust Calum Waddell
Carrie Neil Mitchell
The Company of Wolves James Gracey
The Conjuring Kevin J. Wetmore Jr.
Creepshow Simon Brown
Cruising Eugenio Ercolani & Marcus Stiglegger
The Curse of Frankenstein Marcus K. Harmes
Daughters of Darkness Kat Ellinger
Dead of Night Jez Conolly & David Bates
The Descent James Marriot
The Devils Darren Arnold
Don't Look Now Jessica Gildersleeve
The Evil Dead Lloyd Haynes
The Fly Emma Westwood
Frenzy Ian Cooper
Halloween Murray Leeder
House of Usher Evert Jan van Leeuwen
In the Mouth of Madness Michael Blyth
It Follows Joshua Grimm
Ju-on The Grudge Marisa Hayes
Let the Right One In Anne Billson
M Samm Deighan
Macbeth Rebekah Owens
The Mummy Doris V. Sutherland
Nosferatu Cristina Massaccesi
Peeping Tom Kiri Bloom Walden
Repulsion Jeremy Carr
Saw Benjamin Poole
Scream Steven West
The Shining Laura Mee
Shivers Luke Aspell
The Silence of the Lambs Barry Forshaw
Suspiria Alexandra Heller-Nicholas
The Texas Chain Saw Massacre James Rose
The Thing Jez Conolly
Trouble Every Day Kate Robertson
Twin Peaks: Fire Walk With Me Lindsay Hallam
Witchfinder General Ian Cooper

Forthcoming

[REC] Jim Harper
Cape Fear Rob Daniel
Possession Alison Taylor
Prevenge Andrew Graves

Devil's Advocates

Re-Animator

Eddie Falvey

Acknowledgements

I would like to take a moment to express that I am extremely thankful for the support offered by a large number of people, without whom it would not have been possible to complete this work. First, I would like to start by thanking John Atkinson at Auteur/LUP for taking a chance on me at an early point in my career; his editorial support, advice and friendship has been gratefully received throughout the writing of this volume. I would like to offer a special thanks to Phil Nobile Jr., editor of *Fangoria*, who took the time to talk to me about *Re-Animator*'s impact and legacy, and to Joanna Angel, who spoke to me about her work on the porn parody *Re-Penetrator*.

A great thank you goes to Alice Haylett Bryan who gave me great, encouraging feedback on the manuscript for this monograph, and to the anonymous peer reviewer who supported its progress. I would like to take a moment to thank all the friends and colleagues old and new who have supported this work at various stages of its development, as well as my partner Fiona who graciously and patiently tolerates my love for horror films. I would finally like to thank my family whose love and support continues to be the bedrock on which I maintain my sanity, lest I succumb to a West-esque delirium.

First published in 2021 by
Auteur, an imprint of
Liverpool University Press,
4 Cambridge Street,
Liverpool
L69 7ZU

Series design: Nikki Hamlett at Cassels Design
Set by Cassels Design, Luton

All rights reserved. No part of this publication may be reproduced in any material form (including photocopying or storing in any medium by electronic means and whether or not transiently or incidentally to some other use of this publication) without the permission of the copyright owner.

British Library Cataloguing-in-Publication Data
A catalogue record for this book is available from the British Library

ISBN paperback: 978-1-80085-941-8
ISBN hardback: 978-1-80085-940-1
ISBN epub: 978-1-80085-815-2
ISBN PDF: 978-1-80085-855-8

Contents

Introduction: Re-Animating *Re-Animator* 7

Chapter One: "Interesting little laboratory you have here."

    1980s Horror Cycles and Industry Dynamics 13

Chapter Two: "I suggest you get yourself a pen."

    Watching *Re-Animator* Today 25

Chapter Three: "Don't expect it to tango; it has a broken back."

    Re-Animator and 1980s Horror 39

Chapter Four: "I gave him life!"

    Re-Animator, Stuart Gordon and the Birth of a New Lovecraftian Cycle 59

Chapter Five: "He's Dead?" … "Not Anymore!"

    The Cult Legacies of *Re-Animator* 79

Conclusion: *Re-Animator* Today: The Continuing Cult of a Horror Classic 99

Appendix: Insights into the Landscape of 1980s Horror:

    An Interview with *Fangoria* editor-in-chief Phil Nobile Jr. (2018–) 103

Bibliography 107

Selected Filmography 117

List of Figures and Tables

Figures

All stills from *Re-Animator* and *From Beyond* © Empire International Pictures.

- Figure 2.1 – Cain attempts to revive Megan at the end of *Re-Animator*.

- Figure 2.2 – West faces off against Hill.

- Figure 2.3 – A convergence of splatter horror and sexual threat during *Re-Animator*'s gory finale.

- Figure 3.1 – Jeffrey Combs channeling the pomp and humour of earlier cinematic mad scientists.

- Figure 4.1 – Jeffrey Combs and Barbara Crampton return for *From Beyond* (Stuart Gordon, 1986).

- Figure 5.1 – The contents of Arrow Video's 2017 lavish limited release of *Re-Animator* © Arrow Films.

Tables

- Table 1.1 – An overview of EIP's productions.

- Table 3.1 – A survey of horror releases, 1976-85.

- Table 4.1 – A survey of Lovecraft film adaptation from 1963-present.

- Table 5.1 – A survey of the cult characteristics of *Re-Animator*.

Introduction: Re-animating *Re-Animator*

It is not that Stuart Gordon's *Re-Animator* (1985), a gruesome and blackly comic adaptation of H. P. Lovecraft's 1922 short story "Herbert West–Reanimator", is in search of critical legitimation. Indeed, the film boasts a sustained critical reputation[1] and regularly appears on popular lists of beloved horror films past and present.[2] Here are just a couple of quotes from leading contemporary American film critics that are indicative of the type of praise held for *Re-Animator* upon its release:[3]

> We have been assaulted by a lurid imagination, amazed by unspeakable sights, blindsided by the movie's curiously dry sense of humor. I guess that's our money's worth. (Roger Ebert, *Chicago Sun-Times*, 1985)

> *Re-Animator* has as much originality as it has gore, and that's really saying some-thing. (Janet Maslin, *The New York Times*, 1985)

> [I]t could become a classic of the genre like *Night of the Living Dead* or *Texas Chainsaw Massacre* and enjoy a long life as a cult film. (Kevin Thomas, *Los Angeles Times*, 1985)

Kevin Thomas's review is particularly interesting for his anticipation of the film's future as a cult object. Nevertheless, despite its solid reputation among fans, *Re-Animator* has rarely received the same scholarly attention that has been bestowed on other contemporary horror films. Indeed, in the context of the 1980s horror canon, *Re-Animator* usually sits at the edge of the conversation and is rarely ranked among the decade's horror highlights, where it is overshadowed by the likes of *Alien* (Ridley Scott, 1979), *The Shining* (Stanley Kubrick, 1980), *An American Werewolf in London* (John Landis, 1981), *The Thing* (John Carpenter, 1982), *A Nightmare on Elm Street* (Wes Craven, 1984) and *Evil Dead II* (Sam Raimi, 1987). Film historian Stephen Prince, in his synoptic volume on 1980s American cinema *A New Pot of Gold*, demonstrates this recurring oversight in his overview of the horror genre in which he singles out Kubrick's *The Shining* for textual analysis while stressing the importance of successful horror franchises including *Halloween* (1978–), *Friday the 13th* (1980–) and *A Nightmare on Elm Street* (1984–). *Re-Animator* only appears once in the context of an off-handed reference to horror-comedy. He writes:

> The combination of graphic gore and humor in *An American Werewolf in London*
> proved to be trendsetting. Horror in the eighties often placed ultraviolence and
> mutilation in a cartoonish context and played them for laughs. Sam Raimi's *The
> Evil Dead* (1982) and *Evil Dead II* (1987) and Stuart Gordon's *Re-Animator* (1985)
> epitomized these Grand Guignol comedies. (1999: 303)

While Prince's industry-oriented approach to developments within the horror genre account for part of *Re-Animator*'s impact, its significance extends well beyond its status as a popular horror-comedy. Indeed, per Prince, *Re-Animator* demonstrates a clear influence on the establishment and saturation of horror-comedy as a popular generic hybrid going forward, as well as an excessive gore aesthetic enabled by new and improved SFX techniques that characterised much of the horror films being produced from the mid-1980s onwards. Meanwhile, alongside other mid-1980s horror hits such as *The Fly* (David Cronenberg, 1986), Gordon's film resurrected — or, if I may be so bold, re-animated — the campiness of Golden Age mad science monster films such as *Bride of Frankenstein* (James Whale, 1935), a narrative and tonal tendency that largely fell by the wayside amid the more serious American horror films of the 1970s.

The commercial and discursive strategies that frame *Re-Animator*'s production, release and reception are recurring lines of enquiry for this book. Over the last few decades, scholars working in the field of horror studies have often sought to mount key films as reflections of a particular time and place, occasionally at the cost of overlooking the special role that producers and production companies have in the development of the genre. *Re-Animator* emerged as one of the centrepieces of the short-lived 1980s success of Empire International Pictures, a small-scale production company headed by prolific B-movie producer Charles Band that specialised in trashy genre outputs with an emphasis on horror and fantasy. As the head of Empire International Pictures (and later Full Moon Features), Band produced and/or distributed many of Stuart Gordon's early films. It is my view that this relationship is significant, and that *Re-Animator*'s status as a Empire International Pictures (and, therefore, Charles Band) production reveals much about the aesthetic and economic orientation of production companies in the 1980s. In the context of Empire International Picture's short lifespan, *Re-Animator* was archetypal of the studio's aspirations and commercial manifesto; camp, trashy, witty, gory and with enough cult potential to ensure a future with devoted esotericists with a penchant for

1980s off-beat cultures. Though *Re-Animator* stands apart from most of the studio's other films for its quality, it nevertheless epitomised the sort of product that Empire International Pictures clearly sought to make. If *Re-Animator*'s legacy has a further reach than the other films, then its cult legacy is nevertheless wrapped up with the subcultural appreciation of small-scale production companies such as Band's that is evident in the second life that many of the films have had on home entertainment media.[4]

Furthermore, *Re-Animator* represents the beginning of Stuart Gordon's directing career whose success has been largely indebted to adapting the works of H. P. Lovecraft, a classic American horror author whose influence on fiction, philosophy and popular media is being currently being re-negotiated in light of his archaic and loathsome views on race and gender. Indeed, as of 2015 the World Fantasy Award no longer features the bust of Lovecraft; meanwhile, HBO's recent series *Lovecraft Country* (2020), adapted from Matt Ruff's 2016 novel of the same name, demonstrates a revisionist tendency to salvage Lovecraft's ideas from the author's backwardly racist ideology. Nevertheless, *Re-Animator* remains one of the most popular adaptations of Lovecraft and one that instigated a renewed interest in producing film versions of the author's works (albeit with varying degrees of success); accordingly, in my view, the film's placement within a larger history of Lovecraft adaptations is a key context in which to situate it. Indeed, the volume of Lovecraft adaptations in Gordon's filmography — which include the films *From Beyond* (1986), *Castle Freak* (1995) and *Dagon* (2001), as well as a TV adaption *Dreams in the Witch House* (2006) — recalls a similar degree of sustained interest in a particular author as that exhibited by B-horror auteur Roger Corman in his cycle of Edgar Allan Poe adaptations starring Vincent Price (Gordon too relies often on a familiar cast, not least Jeffrey Combs and Barbara Crampton). Given that Poe and Lovecraft share so many thematic interests, with Poe being one of the most notable influences on the works of Lovecraft,[5] and given the fact that Gordon himself also has two Poe adaptations to his name (*The Pit and the Pendulum* [1991] and *The Black Cat* [2007]), it seems clear that the parallel contexts are worthy of scrutiny. Furthermore, aside from a couple of relatively lightweight surveys of Lovecraftian adaptations – namely Don G. Smith's *H. P. Lovecraft in Popular Culture* (2006) and Andrew Migliore and John Strysik's *The Lurker in the Lobby* (2006) – a comprehensive and academically rigorous history of Lovecraft in adaptation is yet to be completed.[6] Therefore, it will be a further aim of this book to properly situate Gordon's Lovecraft films within a wider history of the author in adaptation.

Both as a Lovecraft adaptation and more generally, *Re-Animator* remains a favourite among horror enthusiasts. Indeed, the film has served as a platform for various modes of cult appreciation since its release in 1985. It was followed by two moderately popular sequels directed by Brian Yuzna (who served as producer on the original film), *Bride of Re-Animator* (1990) and B*eyond Re-Animator* (2003), as well as comic book adaptations and, perhaps most surprisingly, an acclaimed musical that *Variety* called "an entertainment of rich rewards and high accomplishment" (Verini, 2011). *Re-Animator* has enjoyed a series of high-profile releases on home media formats, with prestigious editions available from a variety of international distributors including Anchor Bay, Arrow Video, Second Sight, Selecta Vision and Starz Home Entertainment. It is clear from all these factors that *Re-Animator* has a substantial stake in horror's history, but one that is yet to be fully explored. It is my aim that this book makes good on these sources of interest; that it rectifies *Re-Animator*'s minor presence in existing scholarship by recasting it against a series of key historical, industrial and theoretical contexts relating to the 1980s American horror industry and beyond. In doing so, it is my hope that this book succeeds in cementing *Re-Animator*'s place within horror studies once and for all.

Footnotes

1. On *RottenTomatoes*, *Re-Animator* has received 95% positive reviews from 59 reviewers.
2. A recent list by the staff of *SlantMagazine* places *Re-Animator* at number 64 in its top 100 films (2018), sandwiched between *A Nightmare on Elm Street* at 65 and *The Thing From Another World* (Christian Nyby, 1951) at 63. A similar list by *TimeOut* finds *Re-Animator* at number 93, between *Scream* (Wes Craven, 1996) and *Henry: Portrait of a Serial Killer* (John McNaughton, 1986).
3. That is not to say that *Re-Animator* did not also attract less favourable reviews. In one charmingly dismissive review, David Kehr of the *Chicago Reader* wrote this of the film: "Ludicrous and inept […] It's this kind of flat-footed stuff that gives garbage a bad name" (1985: n.p.).
4. Other notable companies specialising in similar products include Troma (arriving before EIP in 1974) and Trimark Pictures (1989-2001) which emerged in competition with Full Moon Features (1988–).

5. This is directly supported by a letter that Lovecraft wrote in a 1916 letter to Rheinhart Kleiner in which he states that "when I write stories, Edgar Allan Poe is my model" (qtd in Joshi and Schultz 2005).
6. David Simmons's edited collection, *New Critical Essays on H. P. Lovecraft* (2013), does offer some more rigorous scholarship on the topic.

Chapter One: "Interesting little laboratory you have here." 1980s Horror Cycles and Industry Dynamics

Horror Films in Reagan's America

Do we need another book arguing that 1980s America, and American cinema, accounts for a time of tumultuous change? I am doubtful. It has now been over 40 years since Robin Wood influentially made the case that horror films reflected the state of a nation that was wrought with conflicts both at home and overseas:

> Seemingly innocuous genre movies can be far more radical and fundamentally undermining than works of conscious social criticism [...] The old tendency to dismiss Hollywood cinema as escapist always defined escape merely negatively as escape *from*, but escape must also logically be escape *to*. Dreams are also escapes, from the unresolved tensions of our lives into fantasies. Yet the fantasies are not meaningless; they can represent attempts to resolve those tensions in more radical ways than our consciousness can countenance. (1979: 30)

The reflectionist turn evinced by Wood culminated with his reading of 1970s American horror as a simulacrum of the nation's "collective nightmare", a critical position that reached its apex in his proclamation that "what happens in the cinema will clearly depend upon what happens in American society and politics" (1986: 2).[7] Following Wood, a substantial corpus of scholarship emerged making similarly ambitious claims that the nation's social and political circumstances were the primary context for the content of the films produced. One such scholar, Andrew Tudor, essentially reasserts Wood's mantra, writing that "there is no doubt that the modern horror movie, like all popular culture, tells us something about the society in which we live" (2002: 116).

There is no question that horror has at times demonstrated a clear sensitivity to the various signs of the times — see George A. Romero's *Night of the Living Dead* (1968) and its sequels (1978-2009) for an example of a series of films with a clear, and pointedly authorial, critical agenda. Indeed, Gregory Waller writes that *Night of the Living Dead*:

> offers a thoroughgoing critique of American institutions and values. It depicts the

failure of the nuclear family, the private home, the teenage couple, and the resourceful individual hero; and it reveals the flaws inherent in the media, local and federal government agencies, and the entire mechanism of civil defense. (2000: 258)

This is all well and good, but to claim that *all* horror functions as an allusive vehicle for working through contemporary anxieties would be to risk misunderstanding attendant and, even, overriding structures, such as identifiable aesthetic patterns, economic factors and salient commercial strategies.[8] As much as it has proven popular to locate feelings towards particular times and places in the formal and thematic particularities of a given text, sometimes it is worth slamming the brakes on reflective textual analysis to give thought to alternative determining contexts. While the argument that society co-produces film content is a satisfying one, and one that can be neatly applied to certain horror films associated with the Reagan and post-Reagan eras — see, for example, the political and social commentaries of films such as *They Live* (John Carpenter, 1988), *Society* (Brian Yuzna, 1989) and *Candyman* (Bernard Rose, 1992) — a film like *Re-Animator*, with its bawdy display of gore-inducing mad science, is comparatively harder to reconcile within the critical schema of reflectionism (though that isn't to say I won't try to do so in later chapters).

So while there is a neatness to reflective readings that makes them attractive for writers hoping to employ popular culture as a means of deconstructing the past and present world, there are other key factors to consider such as the special role of studios and producers that are demonstrative of the shifting industry dynamics that drive certain types of production. In recent years, the reflectionist critical orthodoxy has been taken to task by Mark Bernard whose intervention attempts to reframe modern horror in industry-appropriate terms. He writes:

> The "Golden Age" of American horror films was ushered in by economic necessity just as much as it was by counter-cultural revolutionary zeal. While the horror films of the times may have indeed represented codified reactions of disillusionment over Vietnam and, later, Watergate, they also represented the Hollywood film industry's efforts to broaden its reach by updating products and marketing them to more viewers. (2014: 46)

Bernard's refutation of reflectionist paradigms corresponds with David Bordwell's substantial (if contentious) proclamation that "ideology doesn't switch on the camera" (2007: 32). It is hardly controversial to counter Bordwell with the claim that no work is created in an ideological vacuum, but it is nevertheless insightful to note that the ideology fuelling film productions can be both economic and born of a desire to offer social criticism. It is clear in work from Wood to the present day that there has been a profound critical economy generated and sustained by reflectionist readings of key films that has been responsible for perpetuating assumptions about the horror genre and its relationship to the wider cultural moment. If the reflectionist critical custom is responsible for viewing horror in a particular way that extricates meaning from political and social contexts, then even the reception of filmmakers with auteur status such as George A. Romero — who is regularly offered up as evidence for the strength of such readings — does not override the need to consider key production dynamics. Indeed, Tom Fallows has argued as much in his incisive assessment of Cambist Films (a small-scale production company with whom Romero collaborated in the 1970s), where he observes a "rare intersection between imported art cinema, exploitation, and quality independent film" (2018: 93). By resituating Cambist Films in the overarching history of independent production-distribution outlets, Fallows presents a clear directive that any reading that can be made for Romero as a socially-conscious filmmaker should not be made at the cost of overlooking the production contexts from which his films emerge.

Even if *Re-Animator* does not automatically lend itself to reflective readings — at least not in the way that, say, one of Romero's *Dead* films, or a later film like *Candyman*, might — I am keen to not offer a book that delivers nothing beside textual analysis, but rather one that pays close attention to the salient factors surrounding the text. It is my view that if scholarship fails to effectively historicise industrial contexts, then it will be at the price of failing to reconcile key economic modalities within our wider understandings of the horror genre, including its role as a force for social commentary. Indeed, film historians such as Jon Lewis have observed "dramatic corporate restructuring" (2007: 352) as a prevailing influence on the outputs of American film in the 1980s; therefore, it is a leading objective of this book, and this chapter in particular, to explore whatever reflective economy *Re-Animator* has beside, and not in place of, its identity as a production of Empire International Pictures, a minor studio exhibiting industrial archetypes that happened to be emerging out of the 1980s American horror market.

B(R)AND RECOGNITION: IDENTIFYING THE ECONOMIES OF 1980s AMERICAN HORROR IN THE FILMS OF EMPIRE INTERNATIONAL PICTURES

Headed up by Charles Band, Empire International Pictures (EIP hereafter) emerged out of the wreckage of Charles Band International Productions, a small-scale production company specialising in the same sort of low-budget genre fare that would later typify EIP's output.[9] With EIP, despite its short life span, Charles Band has rightly been recognised as a major influence on the landscape of 1980s American horror. In a 1987 interview with *Fangoria* magazine, Band laments the radically changed industry:

> It's not like the old days when I first started. In those days, you could shoot a movie in two weeks for $50,000 and make money. It's different now. We can't compete visually with something like *Poltergeist*. But we can compete from a story standpoint. Many big studio pictures are junk. When you have a great story, and a wonderful character who is developed so the audience can identify with him, you're going to have a hit. (qtd in McGee, 1987: 56)

Speaking in largely economic terms – differentiating between "junk" and "hits" – Band demonstrates the ideological backbone of decision-making in the context of small-scale mid-1980s horror. If there was consideration over a film's content, then for Band it directly corresponds with how lucrative those factors could be. Indeed, for Band, *Poltergeist* (Tobe Hooper, 1982) was not a benchmark for the genre for its sophistication or social commentary, but because it made substantial amounts of money.[10] By identifying visual effects as a key reason for *Poltergeist*'s success, Band demonstrates how commerciality and aesthetics pertaining to commercial success were a prevailing consideration for horror producers at that time.[11]

More than a desire to comment on shifting sociopolitical dynamics, what Band's observations illustrate is the fact that horror filmmakers were just as prone to being at the mercy of the box office as filmmakers working in any other genre. In his acknowledgement that "it's different now", Band articulates the increased risks that came with inflated budgets as a result of big-studio competition. Band's thoughts predicate an important question for producers such as himself: if Tobe Hooper, the director responsible for *The Texas Chainsaw Massacre* (1974), one of the most significant (and profitable) independent horror films of the 1970s, is now capable of making commercially-viable studio horror films for the likes of MGM, then in what ways can small-scale producers still compete?

The answer for Band was in product distinction, augmented in the cost-effective provision of quality content as the leading commercial strategy. If the studios, aided by significantly greater capital for budgets, had set their sights on spectacle by way of state-of-the-art effects, then Band was keen to offer competition "from a story standpoint". It is not my aim here to drag Band's filmography through the muck, but it is nevertheless fair to say that the "quality" of his productions was a little hit-and-miss. The matter of quality aside, though, it is hard to fault the prolificness of EIP in general or Band in particular, who pumped out B-movies (or perhaps C-movies) at an impressive rate. Table 1.1 offers a partial overview of EIP's key films, which presents the company as a close-knit community of collaborators.

Year	Film	Director	Producer(s)	Writer(s)
1983	The Alchemist	James Amante (Charles Band)	Lawrence Appelbaum	Alan Adler
1984	The Dungeonmaster	Various (inc. Band)	Charles Band	Various
	Trancers	Charles Band	Charles Band	Danny Bilson, Paul De Meo
	Ghost Warrior	J. Larry Carroll	Charles Band	Tim Curnen
1985	Ghoulies	Luca Bercovici	Jefery Levy	Luca Bercovici, Jefery Levy
	Re-Animator	**Stuart Gordon**	**Brian Yuzna**	**Stuart Gordon, William Norris, Dennis Paoli**
	Savage Island	Nicholas Beardsley	Charles Band, Mark Alabiso	Nicholas Beardsley
	Underworld/ Transmutations	George Pavlou	Kevin Attew, Don Hawkins	Clive Barker
	Walking the Edge	Norbert Meisel	Sergei Goncharoff	Curt Allen
	Zone Troopers	Danny Bilson	Paul De Meo	Danny Bilson, Paul De Meo

1986	Breeders	Tim Kincaid	Cynthia De Paula	Tim Kincaid
	Crawlspace	David Schmoeller	Roberto Bessi, Michael Deak	David Schmoeller
	Eliminators	Peter Manoogian	Charles Band	Paul De Meo, Danny Bilson
	From Beyond	**Stuart Gordon**	**Brian Yuzna**	**Stuart Gordon, Brian Yuzna, Dennis Paoli**
	Rawhead Rex	George Pavlou	Kevin Attew, Don Hawkins	Clive Barker
	Robot Holocaust	Tim Kincaid	Charles Band, Cynthia De Paula	Tim Kincaid
	Troll	John Carl Buechler	Albert Band	Ed Naha
	TerrorVision	Ted Nicolaou	Charles Band, Albert Band, Debra Dion	Charles Band, Ted Nicolaou
1987	The Caller	Arthur Allan Seidelman	Charles Band, Frank Yablans	Michael Sloane
	Creepozoids	David DeCoteau	David DeCoteau, John Schouweiler	David DeCoteau, Buford Hauser
	Dolls	**Stuart Gordon**	Charles Band, **Brian Yuzna**	Ed Naha
	Enemy Territory	Peter Manoogian	Cynthia De Paula, Tim Kincaid	Stuart Kaminsky, Bobby Liddell
	Mutant Hunt	Tim Kincaid	Charles Band, Cynthia De Paula	Tim Kincaid
	Prison	Renny Harlin	Charles Band, Irwin Yablans	C. Courtney Joyner, Irwin Yablans
	Necropolis	Bruce Hickey	Cynthia De Paula	Bruce Hickey
	Slave Girls From Beyond Infinity	Ken Dixon	Don Daniel, Ken Dixon	Richard Connell, Ken Dixon

1988	Catacombs	David Schmoeller	Charles Band, Hope Perello	David Schmoeller
	Cellar Dweller	John Carl Buechler	Charles Band, Bob Wynn	Don Manchini
	Ghost Town	Richard McCarthy	J. Larry Carroll	Duke Sandefur
	Ghoulies II	Albert Band	Albert Band	**Dennis Paoli**
	Pulse Pounders	Charles Band	Charles Band	Charles Band, Paul De Meo, **Dennis Paoli**
	Sorority Babes in the Slimeball Bowl-O-Rama	David DeCoteau	John Schoweiler	Sergei Hasenecz
	Transformations	Jay Kamen	Charles Band, Bob Wynn	Mitch Brian
	The Occultist	Tim Kincaid	Cynthia De Paula	Tim Kincaid
1989	Arena	Peter Manoogian	Irwin Yablans	Danny Bilson, Paul De Meo
	Deadly Weapon	Michael Miner	J. Larry Carroll, Peter Manoogian	Michael Miner
	Intruder	Scott Spiegel	Lawrence Bender, Sam Raimi	Scott Spiegel
	Robot Jox	**Stuart Gordon**	Charles Band	**Stuart Gordon**, Joe Halderman
	Cannibal Women in the Avocado Jungle of Death	J.D. Athens	Gary Goldstein	J.D. Athens
	Dr. Alien/I Was a Teenage Sex Mutant	David DeCoteau	David DeCoteau, John Schouweiler	Kenneth J. Hall
1991	Spellcaster	Rafal Zielinski	Charles Band	Ed Naha, **Dennis Paoli**

Table 1.1 – An overview of EIP's productions (names in bold to highlight recurring appearances by Re-Animator's *central personnel)*

Picture the scene. An intertitle informs the audience the year is 1871. The sequence opens on a woman, Anna, walking alone through a dark, wooded area. Cut to a man, Aaron (played by Robert Ginty, star of cult hit *The Exterminator* [James Glickenhaus, 1980]), searching for her; meanwhile, the score deploys quavering strings, clanging bells and the occasional supernatural orchestral flourish. The shots are poorly framed, the lighting meagre, the acting is equally pitiable. The woman comes across a mysterious man standing next to a fire, looking ominous; the man is DelGatto, the titular alchemist. Anna approaches the man when the scene abruptly cuts back to Aaron, but by the time he reaches Anna she has already fallen under DelGatto's spell. Aaron fights the alchemist, during which he accidentally stabs and kills Anna. The alchemist then puts a curse on Aaron, condemning him to eternity as an animal, before disappearing into the flames. Aaron is left alone in the clearing with Anna's corpse. He attempts to carry her from the forest but collapses. The scene ends with Anna's body rolling out of sight just as Aaron begins his transformation. Then plays the opening credits.

This is the opening of *The Alchemist* (1983), a low-budget horror film about the vengeful victim of an evil magician's curse, Charles Band's debut feature (directed under the alias James Amante) that marked the beginning of EIP's horror output. The film was completed as early as 1981 under the auspices of Band's earlier company, Charles Band Productions, only for its release to be stalled while Band found his feet (and straightened his finances) on the B-movie production circuit. If my description of the film's opening sequence is not enough to clarify it, then I will state for the record that *The Alchemist* is about as close to a prototypical 1980s B-horror film as you can get: cheaply made, trashy, occult-themed (popular in the period), gory and, for the most part, structurally unintelligible. Furthermore, and despite the film's myriad shortcomings, *The Alchemist* offers an impression of what would become EIP's staple product: inexpensive, tongue-in-cheek fantasy-horror films targeting a young audience in search of the cheap thrills. *The Dungeonmaster* (various, 1984) followed in *The Alchemist*'s footsteps, an anthology horror-fantasy film that paid dividends to the popularity of the role-playing game *Dungeons & Dragons*. EIP's next major horror release, *Ghoulies* (1985), was a sizeable hit, relatively speaking, perhaps in part due to its similarity to Joe Dante's fantasy-horror blockbuster *Gremlins* (1984) which beat Band's film to market by six months. EIP's output continued with a series of horror features that included: *Re-Animator, Underworld/ Transmutations, Troll* (all 1985), *Breeders, Crawlspace, Dolls, Dreamaniac, From Beyond, Mutant Hunt, Necropolis, Rawhead Rex, Terrorvison* (all 1986), *Cellar Dweller, Creepozoids, Ghoulies II, Prison* (all 1987), *Catacombs, Ghost Town, Intruder, Spellcaster, Transformations* (all 1988). Many of these films have gone on to enjoy cult status through VHS collecting cultures and DVD and Blu-ray re-releases via the likes of Second Sight, 88 Films, Shout Factory and Arrow Video.

It would be erroneous to suggest that such films were wholly representative of EIP's output which included various types of (largely) exploitation release. One of the first titles acquired for distribution, for instance, is *Walking the Edge* (Norbert Meisel, 1985), a film that illuminates the allusive, small-budget shadow cinema that EIP specialised in producing and/or distributing during the VHS-dominated 1980s. Just as *Ghoulies* finds *Gremlins* transfigured into a budget format, in *Walking the Edge* director Norbert Meisel[12] offers up a *Death Wish*-cum-*Taxi Driver* trip into the realm of conservative urban paranoia and ultraviolence in which the hilariously-named Jason Walk (played by Robert Forster) features as the man on the titular edge. In a manner that is perhaps illustrative of the knowingness expected of viewers, the film bears a comically overstated tagline that reads: "This cabbie ain't askin' for no tips. They drove him to the edge, and on the edge there are no rules." If *Walking the Edge*, a revenge-thriller, is about as close to standard fare as EIP ever would list in their catalogue, then *Savage Island* (Nicholas Beardsley, 1985) represents an altogether different type of exploitation. The film briefly stars Linda Blair of *The Exorcist* (William Friedkin, 1973) in a lowly riff on the women in prison subgenre made successful by popular exploitation filmmakers Jesús Franco and Jack Hill, a distasteful trend of exploitation films that depict scantily-dressed women incarcerated and at the mercy of their often sexually-aggressive captors.

EIP's manifesto for film production clearly depended upon the fleeting value of trashy genre B-movies to a certain type of punter mostly associated with the VHS era. Evidently, Band's studio was working with a particular audience in mind, one who would appreciate (with tongue in cheek) EIP's subversive riffs on popular trends. Consider *Trancers* (Charles Band, 1984), one of the jewels of the EIP crop, a film that knowingly melds *Blade Runner* (Ridley Scott, 1982) with *The Terminator* (James Cameron, 1984) into a small-scale independent hit that Kim Newman calls Band's "masterpiece and one of the liveliest, wittiest, cleverest cheapies ever made" (2015). Situated in opposition to large-scale studio fare, EIP's commercial strategy illustrates the opportunities offered to and provided by a counter-cinema purveying small-scale, fan-friendly exploitation. Jeffrey Sconce has formulated an understanding of the value of such films to fans of trash, writing:

> In cultivating a counter-cinema from the dregs of exploitation films, paracinematic fans, like the academy, explicitly situate themselves in opposition to Hollywood cinema and the mainstream US culture it represents. (2010: 113)

Counter-cinema, then, is an oppositional cinema that capitalises on the aesthetic and political (or markedly apolitical) potential of bad taste filmmaking. Sconce characterises these "paracinematic audiences […] as a disruptive force in the cultural and intellectual marketplace" (372), identifying their countercultural viewing tendencies as wilful resistance to the power of tastemakers.

Janet Staiger's criteria for an independent film studio includes consideration of the following factors: "the relations in its work process, its means of production, the financing of its films, its conception of quality films, and its system of consumption" (2013: 17). It is clear from the survey of EIP's output offered by the table above that most of its films were being produced by a relatively tight-knit group of collaborators including Band himself, as well as Tim Kincaid, George Pavlou, Peter Manoogian, David DeCoteau, and of course Stuart Gordon, all of whom directed multiple films for the studio. Indeed, over the course of EIP's short lifespan, working relationships emerged that would characterise the careers of many of its major players going forward, not least between Gordon, Yuzna and Paoli, *Re-Animator*'s chief creators. Even after EIP's bankruptcy and subsequent collapse,[13] Gordon would continue working with Band under his new label, Full Moon Features, producing similar works for them including *The Pit and the Pendulum*, an Edgar Allan Poe adaptation, and *Castle Freak*, another Lovecraft adaptation that will be explored in more detail in chapter four.[14]

RE-ANIMATOR AS AN EMPIRE INTERNATIONAL PICTURES PRODUCTION

So, what can be gleaned from this admittedly short survey of Empire International Pictures, and what is to be made of *Re-Animator*'s position within its filmography? It is first worth noting that *Re-Animator*'s status as an EIP production has not gone uncontested. Producer Brian Yuzna has been dismissive of the studio's involvement and even launched lawsuits after the film's release to wrestle rights back from EIP, which Yuzna subsequently won (Jay, Dewey, Shumate 2013: 157). Stuart Gordon has been slightly more forgiving of EIP's involvement, stating in an interview that "Charlie [Band] did influence the production in a big way. And his father, Albert, helped with the editing of the movie and had a lot of good suggestions that were incorporated into it; the film was a lot more complicated and he simplified it" (qtd in Jay, Dewey, Shumate 2013: 210).

Regardless of the division of labour, *Re-Animator* sits firmly as "the jewel in Empire's crown" (Jay, Dewey, Shumate 2013: 152) and corresponds in form with much of the studio's output during its brief run in the 1980s. It is quite clear that EIP were working to a quite specific remit, producing cheap, independent genre pictures for the video market (that is, excluding a few limited theatrical runs that were granted to some of their bigger features). Indeed — and I have been building up to this pun — the B(r)and identity that Band and his collaborators developed over the short period of EIP's existence was enough to secure his legacy as one of the chief suppliers — or, dare I say it, auteurs — of low-rent horror films, with the ongoing success of Full Moon Features serving as a testament to that fact.

If anything, *Re-Animator*'s popularity and critical reception was crucial to the expansion of EIP and to Band's increasing status as a key figure within the economy of 1980s horror production. As Band recollects, "1984 to around 1988 […] were definitely the golden years of my career so far" (qtd in Jay, Dewey, Shumate 2013: 122). Bolstered by Band's evergreen optimism for keeping a packed production slate, *Re-Animator*'s success led to a dramatic restructuring for the company. The company relocated from Los Angeles to Rome, taking up residence in the then-abandoned and increasingly dilapidated Dinocitta studio, the former production lot of Italian super-producer Dino De Laurentiis (Jay, Dewey, Shumate 2013: 122-3) following his relocation to the United States, where he went on to produce prestige genre pictures such as *Serpico* (Sidney Lumet, 1973), *Three Days of the Condor* (Sydney Pollack, 1975), *Conan the Barbarian* (John Milius, 1981) and *Blue Velvet* (David Lynch, 1986), as well as horror films such as *Halloween II* (Rick Rosenthal, 1981), *The Dead Zone* (David Cronenberg, 1983), *Manhunter* (Michael Mann, 1986) and *Evil Dead II*. Given Band's rapidly ascending standing as a producer of exploitation, there is something oddly poetic in the fact that Band and company came to occupy the space in which *Barbarella* (Roger Vadim, 1968) was shot, an exploitation urtext if ever there was one. It was there that Band went on to produce some of the studio's biggest hits – including *From Beyond*, *Dolls*, *Arena* and *Crawlspace*, among others – before EIP finally, and sadly, suffered a fate that was all too common for many of the independent production/distribution companies at that time.[15] EIP collapsed just a few years later in 1988 due to irreconcilable financial hardships. Even if the company had no choice but to close its doors on new productions, they had nevertheless secured a legacy that would form the platform for Full Moon Features' success. EIP itself remains a source of cult curiosity for its embodiment of a certain ethos and its attachment to a bygone era; the studio's cult capital is evident in the interest that its films still generate, demonstrated by a range of restorations and special re-releases that many of its key films have been subjected to. All in all, Full Moon Features makes it plain that it was going to take more than a few money-problems to deter Band from his unique, blood-splattered vision for the American horror industry going forward.

FOOTNOTES

7. For a modern example of this mode of analysis, see Linnie Blake, *The Wounds of Nations* (2008), and Mark Steven, *Splatter Capital* (2017).
8. Indeed, one glance over the corpus of works intent on mounting modern horror as a conscious response to 9/11 reveals the extent of this critical legacy.
9. Among the better-known films of Charles Band International Productions is *Parasite* (1982), a film that clearly anticipates what would come later with EIP.
10. Boosted by Spielberg's substantial presence as writer-producer, Hooper's *Poltergeist* was the 8th highest-earning film of 1982 (*BoxOfficeMojo*).
11. This comment also demonstrates a marked return to the attraction-based cinema that characterised the medium in its infancy.
12. Meisel was previously known for softcore productions such as *The Adulteress* (1973), *The Devil Made Me Do It* (1974) and *Mafia Girls* (1975), a porn-parody of *The Godfather* (Francis Ford Coppola, 1972).
13. Several of EIP's final films, including *Arena* (Peter Manoogian, 1989), *Deadly Weapon* (Michael Miner, 1989), *Intruder* (included above), *Robot Jox* (included above) and *Spellcaster* (Rafal Zielinski, 1991), were released after the company's 1988 collapse.
14. Notably, both Stuart Gordon and Brian Yuzna would go on to make films with Trimark Pictures who were specialising in a very similar type of product in the early- to mid-1990s before merging with Lionsgate. Yuzna would direct *Return of the Living Dead III* (1993) for Trimark before returning to collaborate with Gordon on *The Dentist* (1996).
15. For a general overview of the shifting dynamics of American film, see: Paul McDonald and Janet Wasko, *The Contemporary Hollywood Film Industry* (2008). For a special focus on independent films, see Yannis Tzioumakis, *American Independent Cinema* (2017). In another work, Frederick Wasser notably identifies the absorption of smaller outfits during the rise of VHS (2001: 176-84).

Chapter Two: "I suggest you get yourself a pen." Watching *Re-Animator* Today

The Plot

The following is a brief recap of the film's plot, intended for those among you who thought it sensible to read a book dedicated to *Re-Animator* having not watched the film beforehand. In the vein of classic Aristotelian tragedies and of the many Lovecraftian protagonists that front his weird tales, *Re-Animator*'s Herbert West is both brilliant and ambitious to the point of mania. The film opens on West, a student at the Institute of Medicine at the University of Zurich, who has just unsuccessfully attempted to resurrect his then-professor, Dr. Hans Gruber, with his newly created re-animation agent (abbreviated to re-agent throughout the film). Police, medical staff and the dean of the university arrive in time to witness Gruber's gory demise. Against accusations of foul play and possible murder, West famously retorts with Frankensteinian gravitas "No, I gave him life!" before the opening credits play.

West arrives at Miskatonic University, New England, recovering after his failed attempt at re-animation. At the North American institution, West immediately clashes with his new professor, Dr. Carl Hill. West criticises Hill's ideas regarding afterlife and re-animation as being derivative of his former instructor's; Hill responds cattily, promising West that he will never achieve a passing grade in his class. West finds residence with fellow medical student Dan Cain and quickly finds time to convert Cain's unused basement into his personal laboratory where he will conduct his experiments. Cain, meanwhile, is secretly engaged to Megan Halsey, daughter of the medical school's dean, Dr. Alan Halsey; the couple fears that news of their relationship will result in Cain being expelled from the institute. Megan is unnerved by West from their first encounter; her suspicions about West are soon confirmed after she walks in on his attempt to re-animate Cain's pet cat. Cain's feelings over the death of his cat are soon overturned by the realisation of what it is he has witnessed; however, when he confronts Dean Halsey with news of their breakthrough the dean is unconvinced and bars them from the school for fear that they have gone completely mad.

Undeterred by the dean's denial of their work and fear for their states of mind, West and Cain break into school's morgue in order to test West's newly balanced re-agent on a human subject, believing that if they prove to be successful it will restore the dean's faith in their sanity and become the platform for illustrious medical careers. Unsurprisingly, the experiment does not go to plan and the cadaver they selected for re-animation returns to life in a violent fashion. Amid the ensuing hullabaloo, Dean Halsey enters the scene and is quickly killed by the savage, zombie-like corpse that the duo have foolishly brought back to life. Cain becomes increasingly inert with mounting shock, but West manages to subdue the creature, courtesy of a bone-saw. Eager to test his re-agent on a fresh subject, West takes it upon himself to inject Dean Halsey with the serum. As with their previous specimen, Dean Halsey returns as a violent, zombie-like creature. Megan then re-enters the scene and is rendered hysterical by the sight of her now-rabid father.

Fig. 2.1 – Cain attempts to revive Megan at the end of Re-Animator.

Unaware of the nature of the ailment that has so quickly and violently afflicted the dean, Dr. Hill is given full responsibility for his care. Suspecting madness, Hill places Halsey in a cell for overnight observation. As he attempts to perform a lobotomy on him, Hill discovers that his colleague is not mad but rather dead, and has since been re-animated. Hill goes in search of West. Upon finding him, Hill attempts to acquire

West's re-animation agent through blackmail, only to be attacked and beheaded by West in an enraged act of vengeance against the would-be "plagiarist". Drunk on the possibilities of his discovery, West re-animates Hill's body and head. As West interrogates Hill's disembodied head, his un-headed body sneaks up behind West and knocks him unconscious. Hill's body retrieves his head and escapes with West's re-agent. Later, Hill finds himself now able to control Halsey via telepathy, a seeming side effect of his re-animation. He uses his new-found powers to have Halsey's corpse kidnap Megan for him, who he has developed a predatory interest in. Hill straps Megan to an operating table where he strips her naked. In one of the film's more controversial sequences, Megan awakens to find Hill's disembodied head performing forced cunnilingus on her. West and Cain arrive at the morgue to find that Hill has been busy re-animating and lobotomising corpses in a bid to create a small army of telepathically-controlled cadavers. During the fight that ensues, the sound of Megan's voice triggers a paternal response in her father who comes to the trio's aid. Amid the chaos, West manages to inject Hill with a potentially lethal dose of his re-animation agent. Hill's body deforms and attacks West, who demands that Cain save his work as he is pulled towards an uncertain fate. Cain and Megan attempt to escape the morgue, but in the process Megan is attacked by one of the re-animated corpses. Cain attempts to revive Megan in the emergency room but it is already too late. Distraught, Cain turns to West's re-animation agent. In a moment of despair twinned with consuming madness, Cain injects West's re-agent into Megan's recently-dead corpse. Just as the screen fades to black, the audience is left with the haunting sound of Megan as her re-animated corpse begins to scream.

GROSS-OUT BODY HORROR AND THE HAUNTING SPECTRES OF DEATH

It is clear that at a textual level *Re-Animator* offers a plethora of avenues for analysis. Indeed, corresponding with the film's status as an exemplar of the horror-comedy mode that found prominence in the 1980s, which will be discussed at more length in chapter three, Rick Worland writes that:

> *Re-Animator* exemplified the splatter era that exhibited spectacles of bodily

destruction traceable to Grand Guignol productions. But it also adopted the Parisian theatre's strategy of "hot and cold showers" to jolt audiences by chasing violence with sexual titillation, mixing medical horrors and absurdist comedy. (2006: 243)

What Worland identifies is *Re-Animator*'s adoption, or even archetypical establishment, of a horror-comedy formula that ricochets between some of the genre's extreme elements. Capitalising on each genre's biological predisposition to push the interpolated boundaries of extremity and taste, *Re-Animator*'s reworking of the comic format for horrific purposes demonstrates how the affective properties of horror and comedy share common genetic material.

Indeed, in a contemporary review for the *Los Angeles Times*, critic Kevin Thomas intimates towards this overlapping of generic elements, stating that:

> To describe what happens is not merely to spoil the show but to invite a repugnance that the film itself skirts because its makers have been shrewd enough to balance the blood and guts with laughter. The special effects pass inspection yet are so outrageous that you can't take them seriously. "Re-Animator" is therefore not really all that scary, although it's absolutely out of the question for the faint of heart and/or impressionable youngsters; it is rather comically gross in the way that "Animal House" was as a fraternity comedy. (1985: n.p.)

The "repugnance" to which Thomas refers could be taken as a response to any number of graphic sequences to be found in the film. It is nevertheless striking that Thomas observes comparable "gross" elements in both horror-comedies such as *Re-Animator* and in frat-comedies such as *Animal House* (John Landis, 1978). Grossness, which registers for Thomas as a key component of both genres, functions both as a transgeneric marker of excess or extremity, and of the affective experience of viewing material that pushes the boundaries of taste and/or decency. Correspondingly, in a chapter on monsters in the horror genre, Ken Gelder observes how monstrosity destabilises boundaries, writing that it "most often resides at (or is relegated to) the edge of culture, where categories blur and classificatory structures break down" (2000: 81). The same can be said of gross-out, or extreme, examples of genre films that exist at the fringe of the genre proper, and which exhibit a similarly flexible (or monstrous) approach to form.[16] As this book has already intimated, *Re-Animator* shares tropes with a variety of different horror subgenres and cycles that includes: classical horror, and especially Frankensteinian mad science horror; post-Cronenberg body horror; horror-comedy, and especially more reflexive examples of the form; and, now, frat-comedy, for Thomas at least.

In his important work on the topic of horror-comedy, *Laughing/Screaming: Modern Hollywood Horror and Comedy* (1994), William Paul accounts for the ways in which gross-out horror and comedy intersect via the playfulness and physicality that is offered by the excessive formal properties of the two genres. He writes that gross-out films "endowed the people who patronised them with a kind of power – the power to find pleasure in material that was not only offensive to the elite but also excluded the culture of the elite" (5). For Paul, the gross-out as an aesthetic principle offered its viewers the opportunity to rebuke the canon, academy and therefore critics by being pointedly oppositional. Indeed, as Paul sees it, it is this resistance to orthodoxies of quality, value and taste that forms the basis of the viewer's pleasure. While the notion of a disembodied head performing forced cunnilingus on his victim might not be to every viewer's taste, that is also kind of the point; Gordon's bloody and absurdist theatre of horrors is a provocation that is intended to disgust and offend, but with enough reflexivity and self-awareness to offer a critical disquisition on the genre in which it operates.

Graphic violent imagery, or grossness, has central a role to play in *Re-Animator*'s epistemological engagement with its central theme: death. Writing on the excesses of body horror more generally, and of *Re-Animator* as body horror specifically, Xavier Aldana Reyes observes that:

> the inclusion of humour in horror does not preclude an overall feeling of fear. Because the body is inherently interstitial and largely operates without our express cognitive control, certain functions, especially those that are internal, may be both a source of laughter – when displayed histrionically – or of horror – when the excess is so overwhelming that it tips over into the comedic. (2014: 55)

For Aldana Reyes, what qualifies *Re-Animator* as body horror, and what is experienced as "repugnance" by viewers such as Thomas, is the abject imagery of corporal disintegration. For Reyes, *Re-Animator*'s excessive displays of the body's interstitiality, rendered in images of violent, abject corporeality, functions as the basis of the film's "horror".

Building on the work of Sigmund Freud, especially *The Uncanny* (1919), Julia Kristeva conceives of "abjection, or the journey to the end of the night", as she poetically describes it (1982: 58), as the horrors exemplified by one's confrontation with their corporeal reality and, therefore, death. For Elizabeth Gross, abjection (on Kristeva's terms) is "what disturbs identity, system and order, disrupting the social boundaries imposed by the symbolic. It respects no definite positions, or rules, boundaries, or socially imposed limits" (1990: 90). The horrors of body horror, then, are the horrors of abjection, not so much due to graphic violations of the flesh, but rather due to the metaphysical confrontation with death that such imagery evokes. Asbjørn Grønstad, writing on the subject of screen death, observes that:

> Watching characters die on the screen does not primarily induce catharsis, but is a means of imagining, or imaging, that which always already escapes definition in real life. Nothing appears as formless, as monstrously amorphous, as the notion of death. The desire for visualizing it – for giving it a shape through aesthetic form – is therefore epistemic rather than cathartic. (2008: 84)

For Grønstad, filmic images of death are amimetic, not mimetic as they are largely understood to be, and represent an aesthetic coming-to-terms with death's unknowableness rather than a direct reflection of it. Grønstad observes that in spite of death's prominence within the realm of art, it remains an impossible subject to comprehend, and therefore death in art can only ever function as an aesthetic figuration operating in the service of its comprehension. Body horror arguably does this as effectively as any other genre of art; it breaks down the body itself, *the* central structure of human experience, rendering the horrors of mortality in its violent organic decomposition. Perhaps more than any other subject, the core theme of body horror is the metaphysical exploration of mortality through the life-cycles of organic matter, especially, but not limited to, the human body. The extreme or simply gross imagery of *Re-Animator* lends itself readily to critical engagements with the metaphysical lines of enquiry that body horror often invites, its vivid display of corporeal excess speaking to the horrific unknowableness of death while illustrating the (often neglected) value that popular entertainments can offer in tackling ongoing cultural anxieties in unexpected ways.

MASCULINITY IN CRISIS: MAD SCIENCE AND SEXUAL IMPOTENCE IN *RE-ANIMATOR*

(Or, how I learned to stop worrying and give psychoanalysis a spin.)

In service of the film's central theme of man playing God as he attempts to overcome death — an aspect that presents West and Hill as heirs apparent to the legacy of Mary Shelley's Victor Frankenstein and his various intertextual disciples — *Re-Animator* playfully shifts gear from the dramatic to the largely comedic by depicting male ambition as farce, courtesy of the comically over-the-top performances provided by Jeffrey Combs and David Gale as West and Hill. In Sally Robinson's work, *Marked Men: White Masculinity in Crisis*, she writes that:

> Because American masculinity has always been about the freedom to move forward (into the frontier or up the career ladder), blockage is, by definition, a threat. For those who have been nurtured on inalienable rights and "natural" entitlements, blockage must appear particularly threatening. (2000: 137)

Robinson's identification of the threats posed by "blockages" to (white) male expression goes some way towards explaining why masculinity bubbles into eruptive displays of strength (physical, intellectual or otherwise power-based) to satisfy those needful (and markedly fragile) egos whose "rights" have been denied. Robinson goes on to explain how often "emotional release is metaphorically dependent on sexual release and both are premised on a construction of male energies as liquid, material forces that flow through the body" (140). Inversely, it might be likewise construed that a denial of the male ego is equally a rebuttal against sexual powers, that failure in any arena translates as a form of impotence. In many ways *Re-Animator* can be read as a film that is largely about masculinity in crisis, about fragility and impotence. When a child is not given what it wants, it has a tendency to throw its toys from the pram; in the case of adult men, when feelings of entitlement are not satisfied, any violence (whether actual or implied) that manifests is what is commonly referred to as displays of toxic masculinity. In the cosmic carnival of blood-soaked penis measuring that is West and Hill's rivalry, *Re-Animator* offers in many ways the ultimate satire of what can happen when fragile male egos are turned towards toxic displays of one-upmanship.

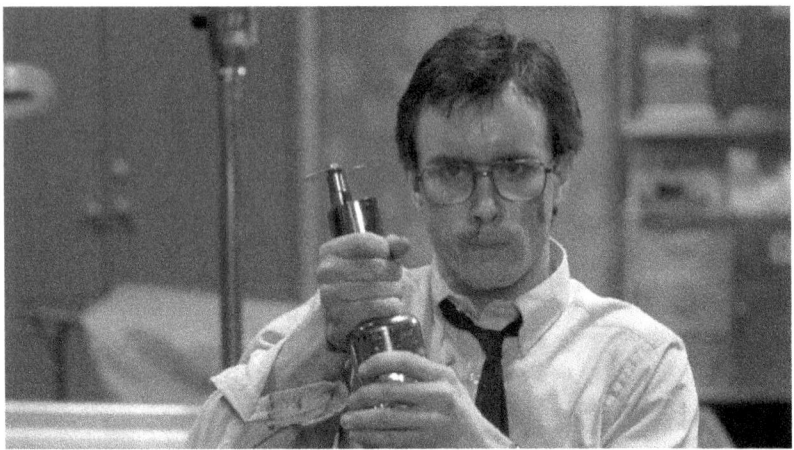

Fig. 2.2 – West faces off against Hill.

In *Re-Animator*, the source of West and Hill's quarrel is intellectual ownership over the re-agent, a viscous liquid (like semen) that is discharged out of cylindrical dispensers (their penises) as proof of their genius (or sexual ability) in a field of scientifically able men. Rhona Berenstein, writing on earlier examples of mad-science horror films, considers the role of gender, stating that "mad-doctor movies are not only male creation fantasy — consider their mothering roles — they are also about anxieties concerning the male body and male bonding" (1996: 123). Correspondingly, Aviva Briefel has observed the sadomasochistic tendencies of the male monster, stating that "his transition from inflicting violence on himself to turning the violence outwards suggests that monstrosity originates when the ability to resist pain turns into a desire to harm others" (2005: 18). West and Hill's "pain", such as it is, manifests in their inability to accept the limitations of their method — an open-ended signifier of sexual competence — which registers for them as an ongoing challenge to their masculinity, or as an edict to achieve results by any (bloody) means necessary.

In the course of West and Hill's violent contestation over their genius, it is notably only

West's outward asexuality that separates him from Hill's outright villainy. That West's pained ego erupts only into violence is distinguishable from the pointedly sexual threat that is posed by Hill's blocked masculinity. Indeed, in a much-discussed sequence, a headless Hill attempts to orally rape Megan who has been bound and spread-eagled on an operating table by her own father, enslaved by re-animation and Hill's telepathy. Slavoj Žižek, channeling Foucault through his preferred Lacanian analytical framework, observes what he calls the fundamentally "'antagonistic' status of sex" (2001: 124). He writes that "'sex' is therefore not the universality, the neutral common ground of discursive practices which constitute 'sexuality', but rather *their common stumbling block*, their common point of failure" (emphasis original, 124). Once again invoking the image of a blockage, Žižek's notion illustrates how sexual violence manifests as a failure to act upon one's sexuality, to do the *thing* the body wants. In the context of Hill's predatory infatuation with Megan, the source of his villainy is both his desire for scientific distinction over West and his involuntary celibacy or impotence,[17] which in the final act erupts as sexual violence against Megan, in a pathetic bid to counter his feelings of inadequacy in both arenas.

It is clear that the sexual and/or reproductive failings of monstrous men have been genetically hardwired into the mad science subgenre. Indeed, Barbara Creed, in a chapter on monstrous masculinity in *The Fly*, writes:

> In the Christian myth, Adam gives birth to Eve from his ribs. The horror film also explores the notion of the male mother/scientist, who attempts to create new life forms in his laboratory, and whose *mise-en-scène* is coded to suggest an intrauterine world. But in his bizarre attempt to usurp female reproductive powers, the male monster of science can only create monsters. Male interest in, and obsession with, birth is explored from a number of perspectives. As the scientist of *The Fly* is re-created as a Brundle fly, coded as female in the text, his genitals drop off. (1993a: 129)

The laboratorial spaces in which West and Hill conduct their experiments are perhaps not so clearly the "intrauterine world" of *The Fly*'s Seth Brundle, yet Creed's suggestion that the laboratory functions symbolically as an unnatural womb works in relation to *Re-Animator* also. The displacement of the mother as a symbol of nature with the father — whose attempts at creation are synthetic and therefore unnatural in the films' logic — is the spark that ignites the violence that concludes both films. Just as the abomination of the Brundle fly illustrates a dangerous upheaval of the natural order of things, West and Hill's crisis is similarly tied to their self-serving male egos, which are in turn guiding them towards the foolish belief that they channel the necessary powers to overcome and master nature.

Both films likewise end in a sequence of sexual annihilation, per Creed's reading of *The Fly*. By the time *Re-Animator*'s phantasmagoric and bloody denouement plays out, Hill's body has mutated beyond recognition into a grotesquely corporeal (yet cosmically Lovecraftian) reproductive abomination, with penis-like tentacles emerging out of his former intestines. Worland describes this monstrosity as "a weirdly phallic yet anal image that culminates *Re-Animator*'s absurdist dance of gore and burlesque" (2006: 251), recognising in the graphic, anatomically-allusive monstrosity that Hill becomes a convergence of sex (or, indeed, sexual failure) with his final destruction. As a(n un)natural punishment for Hill's abuse of Megan, it seems appropriate (albeit in the most macabre of ways) that his destruction culminates in a sequence of monstrous sexual annihilation.

Re-Animator's Scream Queen and the Sexing of Women's Horror Performances

The thematic co-dependence of sex and death in *Re-Animator* mostly coalesces around the character of Megan, played by Barbara Crampton, in a role that would be instrumental to the development of her cult stardom.[18] Despite the fact that the term has historically been deployed in a largely affectionate manner, in the aftermath of feminist revisionism in horror studies (mostly typified by theorists such as Barbara Creed [1993b] and Carol Clover [1992]), the term "scream queen" has the potential to be seen as a reductive simplification of women's involvement within the wider mechanisms of the genre. Indeed, such a term hardly does justice to the more sophisticated performances that are housed within the slasher subgenre. From archetypal star turns including Janet Leigh in *Psycho* (Alfred Hitchcock, 1960), Jamie Lee Curtis in *Halloween* and Sigourney Weaver in *Alien*, to well-respected performances such as those by Heather Langenkamp in *A Nightmare on Elm Street* (Wes Craven, 1984) and Linnea Quigley in *Return of the Living Dead* (Dan O'Bannon, 1985), it is clear that women's roles in horror films have a multitude of components beyond the capacity of the performers to scream. While no doubt popular among horror fans, the latter roles are considerably more neglected when measured against the conventional rubric that determines "great" performances. And yet, such roles nevertheless reflect the clear complexity of women's performances in horror films.

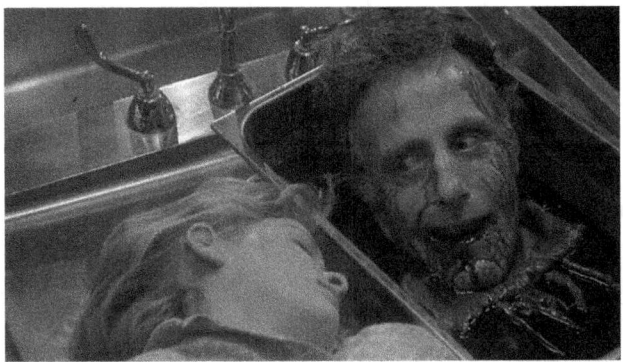

Fig. 2.3 – A convergence of splatter horror and sexual threat during Re-Animator's gory finale.

In a recent turn towards film journalism, Barbara Crampton herself has reflected upon the problems that arise from the term "scream queen". In an article titled "Don't Call Me a Scream Queen", Crampton expresses dissatisfaction at being reduced to a "shrieking damsel" and goes on to explain how the "moniker of Scream Queen is limiting in description and also limiting in its ability to reveal that these actresses are more than the sum of the strain of their vocal cords" (2016: n.p.). Later in the piece, Crampton observes that there is more at work in horror performances, that the real requirement of a "Scream Queen" is less about the screaming per se, and more about the sex exhibited (and often exploited). She laments that, following *Re-Animator*, "I found myself branded a Scream Queen [...] and it hurt to diminish me, to restrict me with a title like this, simply because I embraced horror or my own sexuality" (n.p.). As horror director/actor Axelle Carolyn reiterates, the term does little more than "evoke images of big-breasted helpless victims" (qtd in Crampton 2016). From these assessments, it is clear that sexuality functions as a chief component of "Scream Queendom", and is an aspect that many of the women involved are eager to rebuke. However, upon returning to *Re-Animator*, I am struck by the question: how does the utilisation of this trope shift in accordance with *Re-Animator*'s objective to send-up the genre? In other words, does the film's reflexive intent invite the viewer to reassess how they might approach Megan?

It is certainly the case that any rudimentary overview of Megan's character qualifies her as a "Scream Queen" by ordinary standards: Megan is a striking, voluptuous blonde who is routinely undressed in the film's first act (and again later, during the sexual assault); she spends much of the film dodging unwanted sexual advances from a senior acquaintance, experiencing a series of "daddy" issues by way of her father's death and transformation and, of course, screaming at all the horrors she bears witness to. Indeed, in many ways Megan is the quintessential "Scream Queen", and yet, in the context of *Re-Animator*, a film with pointedly reflexive characteristics, Crampton's performance exhibits parodic daring that could be argued to draw attention to the prosaic mechanisms at work within populist horror filmmaking. Given that the whole enterprise of Gordon's film engenders a symptomatically postmodern, and borderline farcical, rebuttal of the prevailing features and, to some extent, politics of then-contemporary horror (see my psychoanalytical reading above), it seems fitting that the film's component parts should be approached in a manner in keeping with that assessment.

So, the question emerges, how does a "Scream Queen" function in a film that is consciously reformatting horror tropes in order to fulfil both parodic as well as horrific intentions? That Hill's leering over Megan is amusing in its obviousness actually works to demonstrate how sexual threat occupies the horror genre at the base level of form and function. Indeed, in *Men, Women and Chain Saws*, Clover's pivotal work for feminist approaches to horror film, she writes:

> If one holds that the male can never escape the sensations of his own body, the fact remains that in narrative and cinematic imagery, it is the female body that structures the male drama, and to which he assimilates, in his imagination, his own corporeal experience. (1992: 218)

What is established here, especially when paired to the construction of the "Scream Queen" as a staple icon of the genre, is the simple fact that horror films allow for violent, and notably masculine, sexual fantasies to be constantly enabled through the repetition of an internal, generic logic that presents female sexuality as an object to be acquired by force.[19]

It is true that this reading falls down if the film in some way works to address this tired yet prominent generic modal. Even if *Re-Animator*'s finale does not quite amount to a total unshackling of the trope, then there is a conscious acknowledgement of the way in which horror films have been permitted to operate. Unlike West, who retains an appropriately Lovecraftian asexuality over the course of the film, Hill's violent sexual fantasies over Megan are punished with a fate that amounts to sexual annihilation, rendered through the overtly phallic and anal imagery of the monstrosity that he finally becomes.

Of all the films to address the "Scream Queen" trope of the slasher, arguably none have done more work than the original *Alien* franchise (1979-98), in its development of its female protagonist Ripley. As Thomas Doherty points out, *Alien* resists direct replication of the format by "unapologetically affirm[ing] Ripley's strength and tenacity" in spite of the "panties and skimpy T-shirt" that she is put in during the final encounter (1996: 196). In that case, when she returns later as "the well-rounded warrior-woman" (196) of *Aliens* (James Cameron, 1986), a trajectory has been formed from which she has been allowed to evolve out of her (admittedly short-lived) origin as a "final girl".[20] In Ripley's evolution, during which she defeats the outwardly phallic Xenomorph multiple times across the four films in which she features, there are clear attempts to address the limited construction of gender in horror. Unlike the *Alien* franchise, which is largely serious in tone, *Re-Animator* has the added luxury of playing for laughs and, in doing so, is able to address the trope in other ways. So, while Megan is in many ways the inverse of Ripley, there is arguably an equally critical element at work in her parodic send-up of the hapless female victim. If the expressed fetishisation of Megan works as a commentary on the role of "Scream Queens" in the legitimation of violent sexual fantasies, then it is by way of illustrating the ludicrousness and, indeed, toxicity of the trope. Ultimately, *Re-Animator*, like *Frankenstein* before it, works as a biting critique of the male ego made postmodern by its rendering of gender politics in such a way that parodies their construction and punishes their abuse.

FOOTNOTES

16. The key work on extreme horror, in my opinion, remains Steve Jones's *Torture Porn: Popular Horror After Saw* (2013). For more general approaches to extreme film, see Tanya Horeck and Tina Kendall's edited collection *The New Extremism in Cinema: From France to Europe* (2011) or Matthias Frey's monograph *Extreme Cinema: The Transgressive Rhetoric of Today's Art Film Culture* (2016).

17. Individuals representing this type of fragile masculinity and its violent effects have come to be referred to as Incels, a portmanteau of "involuntarily celibate" (Beauchamp 2018). Recently, critical opinion has been divided on the comic book film *Joker* (Todd Philips, 2019) for its supposedly sympathetic presentation of Incel violence (Bundel 2019).

18. Notably, the actor would return to work with Stuart Gordon on further Lovecraftian horrors *From Beyond* and *Castle Freak*, as well as the mid-90s sci-fi actioner *Space Truckers*, a box-office bomb which has since come to enjoy a cult afterlife.

19. I have pursued this topic elsewhere in regards to the textual politics of contemporary women's body horror films including *Teeth* (Mitchell Lichtenstein, 2007) and *Raw* (Julia Ducournau, 2016) (Falvey 2020: 203-24).

20. Clover points out in her conceptualisation of horror's "final girls" (1992: 35-42), "the surname by which she is called, Ripley, owes clear debt to slasher tradition" (40).

Chapter Three: "Don't expect it to tango; it has a broken back." *Re-Animator* and 1980s Horror

Re-Animator in the Context of 1980s Horror

Re-Animator is arguably the best film that Charles Band ever produced. Aided by Stuart Gordon's stylistic direction and more blood than you can shake a disembodied talking head at, *Re-Animator* sits for many among the finest horror films of the decade. But what can we make of its decade? The 1980s were without question a significant period of transition for American film,[21] not to mention horror in particular. Following the crisis and collapse of the auteur-led Hollywood renaissance, a more business-minded New Hollywood emerged that sought to produce nothing but mammoth hits, aided by the availability of newly harnessed ancillary markets ranging from VHS to merchandising and so forth.[22]

Transformations within the American film industry were occurring from the top down. As the wider industry (embodied in the major studios) was being recalibrated, so too were smaller outfits reconsidering and reconfiguring their primary products as well as their modes of production. It is not overstatement to claim that it was a period of industry-wide uprising that led to substantial changes in the landscape of American film once the dust had finally settled. This re-landscaping is evident in the horror industry in the franchise boom of the early 1980s, a shift that is reflective of new economic modalities that had arisen out of the emergent production philosophies that were being employed by the major studios, for which they even had horror blockbusters such as *The Exorcist* and *Jaws* (Steven Spielberg, 1975), not to mention their sequels, to thank. As Mark Bernard has written, "understanding that horror films from the 'Golden Age' were commodities and well suited to the changes and realignments taking place in the film industry in the late 1960s and early 1970s makes it possible to see that the films of the Splat Pack were also marketable in their industrial environment" (2014: 28). Bernard's intervention rightly considers the ways in which industrial forces have governed horror cycles through the 1970s "golden age" and into the modern era.[23] Coinciding with Richard Nowell's historical evaluation of the first run of slashers, *Blood Money: A History of the First Teen Slasher Film Cycle* (2011), and his edited collection *Merchants of*

Menace: The Business of Horror Cinema (2014), this group of works take to task a critical tendency to carry out psychoanalytic analysis of horror audiences for their seeming interest in superficial factors such as violence and sex. Industry-orientated re-evaluations of horror film are now in abundance and are bringing a renewed focus to economic modalities over the reflective nature of a film's content.[24]

For Bernard, the "golden age" of American horror was not the 1930s and '40s, Universal's heyday, but the 1960s and '70s (2014: 27). Even if the 1980s failed to offer horror films with the canonicity and cross-generic significance of the likes of *Psycho*, *Rosemary's Baby* (Roman Polanski, 1968), *The Exorcist*, *The Texas Chainsaw Massacre*, *Jaws* and so forth, then that claim should not stand at the cost of recognising that the 1980s marked a series of significant, path-breaking developments for the genre, as I intend to outline. Below is a survey of the most profitable horror films at the American box office across a period of 10 years (1976-1985) following the tremendous success of *Jaws* in 1975.[25]

Year	Horror Release / Dir.	Studio	Budget ($m)	Box Office ($m)	Rank at U.S. Box Office (#)
1976	*The Omen* (Richard Donner)	20th Century Fox	$2.8m	$48.57m	7
	Carrie (Brian De Palma)	United Artists	$1.8m	$25.88m	17
1977	*The Exorcist II: The Heretic* (John Boorman)	Warner Bros.	$14m	$25.01m	23
	Orca (Michael Anderson)	Paramount	$6m	$14.72m	33
1978	*Jaws 2* (Jeannot Szwarc)	Universal	$20m	$102.92m	5
	Halloween (John Carpenter)	Compass International	$325,000	$47m	8
	Invasion of the Body Snatchers (Philip Kaufman)	United Artists	$3.5m	$24.97m	20
	Damien: Omen II (Don Taylor)	20th Century Fox	$6.8m	$24m	22

1979	The Amityville Horror (Stuart Rosenberg)	AIP	$4.7m	$86.43m	2
	Alien (Ridley Scott)	20th Century Fox	$10.7m	$80.93m	5
1980	The Shining (Stanley Kubrick)	Warner Bros.	$19m	$44.02m	14
	Friday the 13th (Sean S. Cunningham)	Paramount	$550,000	$39.75m	18
	Dressed to Kill (Brian De Palma)	Orion	$6.5m	$31.9m	21
	The Fog (John Carpenter)	AVCO Embassy	$1.1m	$21.38m	31
1981	An American Werewolf in London (John Landis)	Universal	$5.8m	$30.57m	23
	Halloween II (Rick Rosenthal)	Universal	$2.5m	$25.53m	30
	Ghost Story (John Irvin)	Universal	N/A	$23.37m	34
	Friday the 13th Part II (Steve Miner)	Paramount	$1.25m	$21.72m	35
	The Final Conflict: Omen III (Graham Baker)	20th Century Fox	$5m	$20.47m	36
1982	Poltergeist (Tobe Hooper)	MGM	$10.7m	$76.61m	8
	Friday the 13th Part III (Steve Miner)	Paramount	$2.3m	$34.58m	21
	Creepshow (George A. Romero)	Warner Bros.	$8m	$21.02m	37
	The Thing (John Carpenter)	Universal	$15m	$19.63m	42
	Halloween III: Season of the Witch (Tommy Lee Wallace)	Universal	$2.5m	$14.40m	53
	Amityville II: The Possession (Damiano Damiani)	Orion	$5m	$12.53m	61

1983	Jaws 3-D (Joe Alves)	Universal	$18m	$45.52m	15
	Psycho II (Richard Franklin)	Universal	$5m	$34.73m	20
	Twilight Zone: The Movie (various)	Warner Bros.	$10m	$29.45m	25
	Cujo (Lewis Teague)	Warner Bros.	$8m	$21.16m	34
	Christine (John Carpenter)	Columbia	$10m	$21.02m	35
	The Dead Zone (David Cronenberg)	Paramount	$10m	$20.77m	37
1984	Ghostbusters (Ivan Reitman)	Paramount	$30m	$229.24m	2
	Gremlins (Joe Dante)	Warner Bros.	$11m	$148.17m	4
	The Terminator (James Cameron)	Orion	$6.4m	$38.37m	21
	Friday the 13th: Final Chapter (Joseph Zito)	Paramount	$2.6m	$32.98m	26
	A Nightmare on Elm Street (Wes Craven)	New Line	$1.8m	$25.50m	40
1985	A Nightmare on Elm Street 2: Freddy's Revenge (Jack Sholder)	New Line	$3m	$29.99m	30
	Fright Night (Tom Holland)	Columbia	$7m	$24.92m	35
	Friday the 13th Part V (Danny Steinmann)	Paramount	$2.2m	$21.93m	41
	Return of the Living Dead (Dan O'Bannon)	Orion	$4m	$14.24m	59
	Day of the Dead (George A. Romero)	United Film	$3.5m	$5m	115
	The Company of Wolves (Neil Jordan)	Cannon	$2.3m	$4.39m	118
	Re-Animator (Stuart Gordon)	**EIP**	**$900,000**	**$2.02m**	**140**

Table 3.1 – A survey of horror releases, 1976-85 (bold to highlight Re-Animator)

Table 3.1 offers a relatively comprehensive overview of the way in which the horror industry was evolving over a crucial ten-year period that led to *Re-Animator*'s release in 1985. For all the canonising discussions of "golden ages", what emerges here are the following things: firstly, evidence that horror continued to be big business for the industry; and, secondly, that its fundamentals were gradually changing. It should be no surprise to see that most of the biggest horror hits of this period come from the major studios (20th Century Fox, Warner Bros., Universal, Paramount) given their increased resources that manifest in the use of established artists, quality effects and widespread marketing.[26] What also emerges from this data, however, is evidence of a granular shift away from horror blockbusters towards horror franchises with a tendency of returning big money from small budgets (see the *Omen, Halloween, Amityville Horror, Friday the 13th* and *Nightmare on Elm Street* franchises). While some of those franchises are notably aided by the resources of a larger studio (*The Omen* at Fox; *Friday the 13th* at Paramount), there is a clear move towards smaller horror productions in the period of VHS's establishment as a new, and key, form of horror consumption.

The cultural legacy of *Re-Animator* is a topic I will return to in chapter five, however it is worth taking a moment to complicate the data offered by the table above, given that *Re-Animator*'s success pales beside the box office revenues of some of the other films included. With a little over $2 million dollars to its name in theatrical takings, it would be fair to say that, while profitable, *Re-Animator* did not set the industry on fire in the way that, say, *A Nightmare on Elm Street* did. And yet, it is important to consider the shifting dynamics of horror consumption against these figures, namely the move towards home releases, of which *Re-Animator* had many. This data, while often hard to acquire, does much to overturn the economic orthodoxy that privileges theatrical takings as the ultimate marker of a film's success. It is important, therefore, to complicate the data above by taking into account *Re-Animator*'s substantial success on home formats, success that owed much to *Re-Animator*'s status as a critically acclaimed release that was equally championed by fan-centric horror publications such as *Fangoria*.[27] As aforementioned, *Re-Animator* has been subject to various home entertainment iterations. To this day, it remains a highly collectable title on VHS, with certain ex-rental copies selling on eBay for as much as $50 each. Indeed, as Jonathan Wroot and Andy Willis observe, there is still much work to be done on the release strategies of cult media and how they represent new and evolving modes of distribution that continue to shape the reception of the films in question (2017: 1-10). It is clear that collecting cultures, historically and presently, have had a substantial role to play in the development of the film's cult capital within horror discourse and across various media platforms.

FROM SLASH TO SPLAT

It is important to consider the economies of 1980s horror, past and present, as a platform for understanding *Re-Animator*'s sustained cultural, subcultural and transcultural significance. While *Re-Animator*, if separated out into its elemental parts, ostensibly belongs to many horror traditions, it is also something of an anomaly in the context of the period's biggest players. By the early 1980s, the template for success within the horror market was John Carpenter's 1978 box office behemoth *Halloween*, arguably the single most important American horror film for understanding the landscape of horror in the 1980s. While no doubt indebted to preceding films such as *Psycho* and 'stalk-and-slash' films associated with the Italian *giallo* subgenre, *Halloween* nevertheless offered new economic possibilities for horror within a late-1970s American context. *Halloween*'s box office takings of $47 million amount to almost 145 times its modest budget of just $325,000. When considered beside a major studio film from the same year, such as Warner Bros.'s *Superman* (Richard Donner, 1978), for instance, which took $134 million against a $55 million budget, one can observe which of the two represents the real success story. In fact, measured as a budget-to-box office ratio, *Halloween* remains one of the most profitable films of all time, on a list that notably includes other horror films such as *Night of the Living Dead*, *The Blair Witch Project* (Daniel Myrick and Eduardo Sánchez, 1999) and *Paranormal Activity* (Oren Peli, 2009) (qtd in Rowles 2010: n.p.).

Importantly, another film that features on that list is *Friday the 13th* (Sean S. Cunningham, 1980). While few of *Halloween*'s imitators offered a similar level of restraint to that employed by Carpenter's seminal slasher, the model certainly endured. If the original *Halloween* was paradigmatic of a new type of American horror film, then the *Friday the 13th* franchise configured it into a replicable commercial model to be taken up by a number of studios with their sights set on franchise success. Andrew Tudor has observed this lineage:

[The first three *Friday the 13th* films] use *Halloween*'s mixture of tension-building, frenzied killing of isolated victims and an increasingly predictable quota of female nudity and love-making, though marshalled together in an altogether cruder fashion than in *Halloween*. Nevertheless, the fundamental situation is that of the terrorizing psychotic, and all the films climax with the pursuit of the solitary surviving female. The threat articulated here, then, is that of an omnipotent human predator, seen at its most intense (though not exclusively) in situations of male-upon-female pursuit. It is rare to find this subtext of male predator and female prey foregrounded, however, so the potential identification of sexual and physical violence remains largely submerged. (1991: 69)

Tudor's analysis would eventually pave the way for important work on gender in the horror film, including that of Carol Clover who took to task gender relations in modern slashers. Just as important, however, is Tudor's recognition of a newly viable economic model indebted to *Halloween*'s success. Indeed, the slasher boom, sometimes identified as yet another "golden age" between 1978 and 1984,[28] saw the release of a range of slasher films that illustrate Tudor's criteria, including *Friday the 13th*, *Prom Night* (Paul Lynch, 1980), *My Bloody Valentine* (George Mihalka, 1981), *The Dorm that Dripped Blood* (Stephen Carpenter and Jeffrey Obrow, 1982), *The House on Sorority Row* (Mark Rosman, 1983), *Sweet Sixteen* (Jim Sotos, 1983), *Sleepaway Camp* (Robert Hiltzik, 1983), *Splatter University* (Richard W. Haines, 1984), *Silent Night, Deadly Night* (Charles E. Sellier Jr., 1984) and *A Nightmare on Elm Street*.

If the taste for slashers had started to wane by the mid-1980s, then what arrived in their place? Well, in 1984, at the end of the slasher's "golden age", the biggest earners on the horror market were two comparatively more family-oriented hits: *Ghostbusters* (Ivan Reitman, 1984) and *Gremlins*.[29] If the levels of gore offered by these major studio productions sets them apart from the blood-drenched theatrics of *Re-Animator* (which followed in 1985), then it is for their shared lightness of touch that these films overlap. Beyond tongue-in-cheek knowingness, an intertextual affect that Philip Brophy has referred to as "horrality" (1986: 2-13), the slashers were often viewed as unpleasant, morally murky films whose appeal seldom extended further than the gratuitous levels of violence and nudity that they offered. The turn towards horror-comedy proved significant. While horror-comedy was not entirely absent from American horror —

see, for example, *Young Frankenstein* (Mel Brooks, 1974) and, later, *The Evil Dead* and *Creepshow* (George A. Romero, 1982) — the success of *Ghostbusters* and *Gremlins* certainly provided substantial evidence of the subgenre's viability. Their success led to a string of tonally lighter horror films, including such hits as *Fright Night* (Tom Holland, 1985), *Re-Animator*, *The Return of the Living Dead*, *The Stuff* (Larry Cohen, 1985), *Night of the Creeps* (Fred Dekker, 1986), *The Little Shop of Horrors* (Frank Oz, 1986), *Bad Taste* (Peter Jackson, 1987), *Evil Dead II*, *The Lost Boys* (Joel Schumacher, 1987), *The Monster Squad* (Fred Dekker, 1987), *The Witches of Eastwick* (George Miller, 1987), *Child's Play* (Tom Holland, 1988) and *Beetlejuice* (Tim Burton, 1988), which all capitalised on the changing tastes evident in the latter years of the decade.

Comedy of Terrors: '80s Horror, Reflexivity, and Gore Aesthetics

> The thing I have found is that you'll never find an audience that wants to laugh more than a horror audience – Stuart Gordon (qtd in Wiator 1992: 84)

This section seeks to explore the rise of the horror-comedy as a significant component of the wider corpus of 1980s American horror film. Indeed, while much ink has been spilled on the curious and controversial case of the slashers, significantly less attention has been given to horror-comedies, a significant mode that emerged in the wake of the slasher's demise. For a book on *Re-Animator*, the development and saturation of horror-comedy is a significant context for its success. Although this aspect of 1980s horror has not gone wholly unnoticed – indeed, Andrew Tudor has observed "the linking of comedy to splatter" (2002: 107) – horror-comedy, despite its prominence at various points in the genre's history, seldom features anywhere beyond the margins of horror studies.

Re-Animator bears the fruits of a range of tropes from preceding horror traditions, not least the splatter aesthetic of horror auteurs — or goreteurs — Herschell Gordon Lewis and, later, David Cronenberg. The success and influence of *Re-Animator* registers it as a key film for the development of the horror-comedy cycle that by the mid-1980s was gaining momentum.[30] Linking these two contexts, *Re-Animator*'s bloody yet funny deployment of gruesome death spectacles and wry jokes was paradigmatic of a new form of spectatorship growing among horror fans that was marked by self-conscious reflexivity and which remains a feature of the genre to this day.[31] Coinciding with improvements in special effects and changing tastes for violence, the formation and saturation of a 1980s gore aesthetic proved a catalytic event in horror's development. Preceding films like Peter Jackson's *Bad Taste* and Sam Raimi's *Evil Dead II*, *Re-Animator* proved emblematic of a modal shift towards gore and laughs over the seriousness that characterised much of recent American horror. And while gore would remain, as it had since the 1960s, a mainstay of the modern genre — especially in the saturation of the torture porn subgenre after *Saw* (James Wan, 2004) — key to the success of *Re-Animator* and its horror-comedy contemporaries were the comedic elements comprised of reflexivity, irony and humour. Indeed, following William Paul's work on horror-comedy, touched upon in the previous chapter, film cognitivist Noël Carroll has tried to makes sense of the relation between these two outwardly oppositional genres, claiming that an explanation of their difference "is made philosophically urgent insofar as it appears that horrific figures and humorous ones can, in principle, be perpetually indiscernible" (1999: 147). Carroll's philosophical curiosity stems from the affective rupture that occurs when a character that, in certain contexts, strikes fears in some viewers prompts amusement in others — take, for example, the various incarnations of Frankenstein's monster.

One element that is worth considering in relation to all this is the increased subcultural literacy of horror fans. As a more "educated" fandom emerged — illustrated by the popularity of devoted magazines such as *Fangoria* (1979–2016 and then 2018–) — it became clear that horror fans imagined themselves differently to those fans committed to other genres. As evidenced by the cycle of horror-comedies that found an audience in the mid-1980s, there is clear currency in a familiarity with the genre's inner workings, and a desire to laugh at the ludicrousness of it all. More than parody or pastiche, horror-comedies such as *Re-Animator* and *The Return of the Living Dead* sacrificed nothing in terms of horror's primary affective qualities such as shock and gore; nevertheless, such films sought to shock while simultaneously making light of the internal machinations of the genre which are recast with a sense of irony (but no less affection). These films scrutinised the familiarity of common plot points and character dynamics; they encouraged viewers to predict and even encourage the bloody fates of the principle characters; they found currency in wry, gallows humour; and, importantly, they offered a critical mass of blood and gore that tipped the pendulum back and forth between disturbing and laughable.

Today, such intertextual tactics might be referred to as the basis of meta-horror, but at the time Philip Brophy coined the term "horrality" to explain a mounting self-consciousness that was becoming increasingly evident in the production and consumption of mid-1980s horror. Ultimately, the hybridisation of these oppositional genres was made possible by three key elements:

- A familiar, knowing audience;
- A genre ripe for deconstruction and/or parody;
- The rise of improved special effects.

It would be an oversight not to consider how these three salient features of 1980s horror-comedy correspond with one another. As current *Fangoria* editor-in-chief, Phil Nobile Jr., pointed out in our correspondence, included in this book as an appendix, the special effects artists of the period "were like rockstars" and, as such, commanded space in the pages of *Fangoria* and other contemporary publications similarly to how Mick Jagger and Keith Richards would occupy the pages of tabloid music magazines. Indeed, *Re-Animator* inspired a 4-page article in that vein in issue 46 of *Fangoria* that emphasised the effects that went into the film's goriest elements.[32] Ernest Mathijs has previously written on the ascension of the special effects rockstars, stating that "it was in the early 1980s that horror effects in particular were deemed important enough to become a legitimate and respected agent in the critical and academic discourse on the horror film" (2010: 153). Preceding horror, by practical necessity as much as by design, employed a restrained approach to gore that typified much of what James Kendrick calls "the gritty, socially provocative horror films of the politically embattled 1970s" (2017: 310). Due to their tendency to favour social commentary over simpler, violent delights, it is unsurprising that 1970s horror films veered away from bloodshed in favour of sustained atmospheres of dread; even the major 1970s slasher films, such as *The Texas Chainsaw Massacre* and *Halloween*, are considerably less bloody than most people remember them to be, or their sequels are. Nevertheless, as the slasher cycle progressed, it reignited a taste for bloodshed before 1980s horror-comedies ricocheted to another extreme, offering such an abundance of gore that viewers retched shortly before laughing at the absurdity of it all, as in the case of *Re-Animator*.

The treatment of special effects artists as auteurs in their own right coincided with a new "scholarly" approach to horror that developed with its popularity in the video age, and certainly when DVD special features allowed viewers to increase their level of knowledge.[33] As Barbara Klinger writes, "media industries attempt to appeal to the collector as a film industry insider, privy to a secret world of information about filmmaking. Insiders have obtained apparently special knowledge possessed by relatively few others" (2006: 68). Despite the generality of Klinger's statement, which is intended to apply to various forms of ancillary media, the existence of magazines such as *Fangoria*, which offered back-lot perspectives on horror filmmaking, provided discursive legitimacy for those fans wanting to go the extra distance and stake their claims as genre aficionados. Before the age of DVD special features, magazines such as *Fangoria* offered the kind of privileged "insider" knowledge that Klinger identifies.

It is for this familiarity that these viewers might register themselves — and, therefore, be registered among their peers — as the sort of genre experts that can recognise and enjoy the pleasures that horror-comedies provide via intertextuality. Bruce Kawin has recognised pronounced forms of reflexivity as a salient feature of horror-comedies in his introduction to the subgenre by way of Mel Brooks's *Young Frankenstein*:

> *Young Frankenstein* gets many of its laughs by making reflexive jokes, trading on the audience's familiarity with every bit of the Universal Frankenstein series. Many aspects of the story are put in a parodistic context or a raunchy one. It is often the clash of tones that provokes the laughter, the inappropriate or surrealistic meeting of over-the-top comedy and horror. But the film is not just a parody; it is also an homage. (2012: 199)

There are important aspects to Kawin's analysis here. First, he identifies that horror-comedy is founded upon recognition and familiarity, of a reflexive interface between horror's past forms and present reception. And second, that such films are not mere parodies, but homages. Indeed, *Young Frankenstein*'s status as an homage is evident in its utilisation of the same sets and props as Universal's original film, reconfiguring the spaces of classic horror production as sites of deconstruction. Despite boasting significantly more gore than Brooks's earlier film, *Re-Animator* offers a splatter-filled homage to the mad science subgenre to which *Frankenstein*, in its various incarnations, belongs. In *Re-Animator*'s central villains West and Hill – played with mad-eyed, campy abundance by Jeffrey Combs and David Gale – Gordon's film doubles down on its reverential throwback to horror's history (Brophy's "horrality"). For some critics, Combs's West displays genetic evidence of intertextuality in his very performance, which Paul Attanasio describes as a "fey psychotic in the Anthony Perkins mold" (1985: n.p.). Likewise, Gale's Hill functions as a Karloff-esque supervillain that harks back to Universal's golden age of monster movies. In various ways *Re-Animator* fits Kawin's description of an homage. Gordon's film successfully channels the ostentatious spirit of the mad science horror films of the past with the comedic reflexivity of the then-present, reinforced by the more recent appeal of a pronounced gore aesthetic. The result is a film that has one foot in the past and one foot very much in the present – a re-vamped, re-configured *Frankenstein* for an age when horror's primary modes, affective properties and cultural currency were undergoing radical changes.

FRANKENSTEIN'S MONSTERS AND THE NEO-BAROQUE: A CINEMATIC LEGACY OF MAD SCIENCE

Andrew Tudor notes that by the end of the 1970s "the Frankenstein tradition [was] in full retreat", observing that by the time the 1980s came around "science [had] become the servant of other interests, and the 'price of progress' — the key issue for fifties mad science — no longer [had] any meaning or relevance" (1991: 150; 152). Ironically, Tudor's period of interest ends in 1984 – if he had held on for just one more year before pronouncing the death of mad science horror films, he would have had no choice but to consider the release of *Re-Animator*, a film that quite clearly frustrates his conclusions. Coinciding with the rise of horror-comedies which traded in the intertextual currency provided by the referential and reverential treatment of horror's past, the resurfacing of mad science horror is evident in Gordon's revitalisation of the Frankenstein mythos in a contemporary format. Alongside Stoker's *Dracula*, Mary Shelley's *Frankenstein* is arguably the other horror narrative that has most significantly shaped the genre's development in films. Indeed, as is evidenced by the horror canon at present — not to mention the current explosion of superhero media, which regularly employ the tropes of mad science horror — the transcultural utility of *Frankenstein*, and the mad science genre more generally, is longstanding.

Fred Botting, in his introduction to monstrosity in *The Handbook to Gothic Literature*, extracts from two lines of Alexander Pope's *Essay on Man* (1733-4) a critical approach to the symbolic utility of monstrosity. For Botting, the lines from Pope — "Vice is a monster of so frightful mien. / As, to be hated, needs but to be seen" (ll. 217-8) — imbues monstrosity with a critical function, utilising it as a visual signifier of disruption to largely abstract systems of human enterprise such as progress and morality. He writes: "as visible demonstrations of vice, monsters displayed — and cautioned readers against — indulgence in improper behaviour, thereby emphasising the benefits of virtuous conduct and signalling the proper — disgusted — reaction to examples of vice" (1998: 163). It is surely no accident that, by the rubric of gothic monstrosity, much of the commentary provided by novels such as Mary Shelley's *Frankenstein* was directed towards men and their debilitating thirst for power. The persistence of this narrative, expressed across a wealth of fictional works — and not ending with *Frankenstein*, but incorporating Victorian fiction as well, including Robert Louis Stevenson's *The Strange Case of Dr. Jekyll and Mr. Hyde* (1886) and H.G. Wells's *The Island of Dr. Moreau* (1896), among others — generates anxiety regarding improper uses of science (and/or magic) by megalomanic men corrupted by their own ambitions.

Indeed, in non-fiction, even, a reactionary discourse against the moral corruption instilled by the scientific/machine age was fast developing, expressing anxieties over the impact of capitalism and industrialisation. Philosopher Thomas Carlyle mounts such an argument in his 1829 essay "Sign of the Times":

> Men are grown mechanical in head and in heart, as well as in hand. They have lost faith in individual endeavour, and in natural force, of any kind. Not for internal perfection, but for external combinations and arrangements, for institutions, constitutions — for Mechanism of one sort or other, do they hope and struggle. Their whole efforts, attachments, opinions, turn on mechanism, and are of a mechanical character. (qtd in Himmelfarb 2007: 36)

The mechanisation of man that Carlyle fears in "Sign of the Times" is played out *in extremis* in fictional works that make monstrous the scientist's demise. For Carlyle, industrial mechanisation (or capitalism) has made mechanical the head, heart and hand of those invested in progress at whatever cost. What Victor Frankenstein, Edward Hyde and Dr. Moreau represent in those aforementioned works is a point of rupture between one's progress and one's humanity.

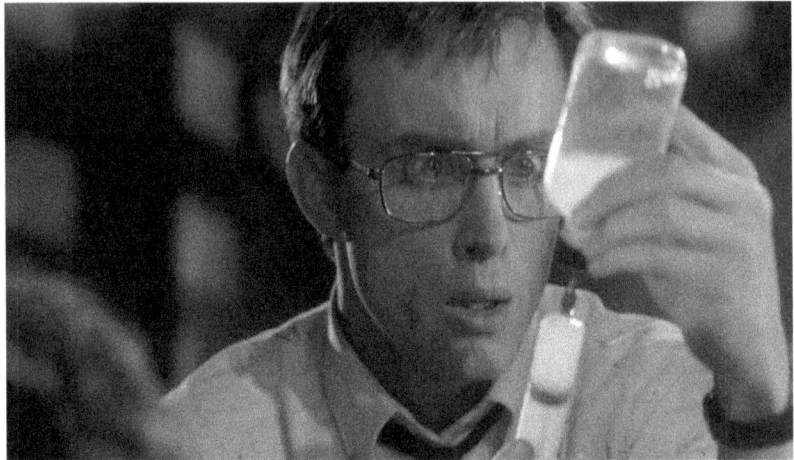

Fig. 3.1 – Jeffrey Combs channeling the pomp and humour of earlier cinematic mad scientists.

With the release of *Re-Animator* in 1985 (as well as EIP's *Transmutations*, another mad science horror film), followed by *From Beyond* in 1986, there was textual evidence that the studio showed recurring interest in revitalising the waning subgenre. By the time that David Cronenberg triumphed at the box office with his gory update of *The Fly* in 1986, the taste for mad science horror films had clearly been restored. Coinciding, no doubt, with the increased genre literacy that I identified in the section above, the return of mad science demonstrates how recognisable intertextuality (evident in the subcultural currency of horror's past) emerged as a key resource for 1980s horror. The more successful of these mad science reimaginings, *Re-Animator* and *The Fly*, succeeded in capitalising on the enduring currency of horror's own canon and, in doing so, mined and repurposed the genre's deep past to provide stock for its present. As new economic and cultural modalities continued to emerge, and the exchange rate of the subcultural capital of classic horror was on the rise, the return of mad science horrors represented a convergence of old and new that illustrated some of the directions in which American horror was moving.

Xavier Aldana Reyes situates *Re-Animator* in relation to the twin legacies of *Frankenstein* (a literary precedent) and body horror (largely filmic) (2014: 65-74). In his chapter on the gothic elements of body horror, Aldana Reyes writes:

> In *The Fly*, monstrous corporeality is first embraced for its fascinating abjection, for the alternative visual and bodily landscapes it suggests, but is ultimately feared for the loss of humanity it entails. Body horror capitalises on this blurring of boundaries to generate both affect and interest. In *Re-Animator*, the fear is situated in a similar place: in the indiscernible areas where bodies stop being alive, yet carry on living. (2014: 73)

In these two key texts of the mad science revival, Aldana Reyes comes to understand their presentation and treatment of the horror body as a manifestation of the primary themes of corporeal abjection, existential fear and the uncanniness of re-animation. In his analysis of Cronenberg's cinema more generally, Aldana Reyes offers a continuation of a common reading, that his cinema "literalises the horrors of embodiment", represented by infection and subsequent disintegration, claiming that "the visceral quality of the mode [that is, body horror] is both played with at a surface level and dissected at a structural one" (58). It seems possible to expand one key aspect of Aldana Reyes's analysis here: the work of "play" in the reproduction of familiar textual elements. Indeed, Aldana Reyes's choice of verb reaffirms the indebtedness of such films to earlier horror formats while signposting the tongue-in-cheek-ness of the texts under discussion. On the one hand, you have *Re-Animator*, an adaptation of a Lovecraft short story with textual antecedents in Shelley, and after it, *The Fly*, a gorier update of a popular 1950s B-movie. Discounting for a moment the textual and industrial parallels between Gordon's Lovecraft adaptations and the Corman and Price cycle of Edgar Allan Poe adaptations in the early 1960s — a topic to be saved for chapter four — there arise tangible markers that horror filmmakers were consciously cashing cheques on a lucrative subcultural rate of exchange, finding purchase in repeated cycles of production in their utilisation of horror's past to inform its present.

The revival of mad science horror films is suitable evidence of horror's cyclicality. In his seminal essay on the cognitive pleasures of horror films, entitled "Why Horror?" (2002: 33-46), Noël Carroll identifies what he perceives to be key narrative elements to the genre's construction and success. For Carroll, horror's narrative pleasures mostly circulate the icon of the monster in its many forms:

> The horror story is driven explicitly by curiosity. It engages its audience by being involved in the processes of disclosure, discovery, proof, explanation, hypothesis, and confirmation. Doubt, skepticism, and the fear that belief in the existence of the monster is a form of insanity are predictable foils to the revelation (to the audience or to the characters or both) of the existence of the monster. (2002: 35)

Even if Carroll's account fails to factor in the affective intensities of the genre, which are often actively sought out by its audience(s), then it nevertheless succeeds in illustrating how narrative tropes have traversed a range of cultural and/or industrial contexts. The disclosure and discovery archetype that Carroll identifies forges a clear link between horror's past and present, recognising the transcultural utility of particular narrative practices, not least the mad science format that draws a trajectory from Shelley's *Frankenstein* to Lovecraft's short story to Gordon's 1985 adaptation, each expressing their own cultural elements.

Angela Ndalianis positions *Evil Dead II*'s recognisable intertextuality in relation to the neo-baroque to consider the ways in which the film signifies "an accumulation of monadic units […] the (neo-)baroque invites the audience to contemplate the relationship between the one and the infinite series, or the whole, while also considering the way intertextual ruins from the past can be recombined to create a new entity" (2004: 79-80). Ndalianis's analysis dismisses the notion that texts exhibiting neo-baroque elements can be readily dissected according to distinct, traceable forms of intertextual correspondence, suggesting that they are in fact more complicated. Indeed, if one uses theories of intertextuality as a critical tool with which to approach the composite structure of "the text" in its entirety, then such readers will find those texts to be resistant to superficial forms of analytic disentanglement — quite frankly, there is more going on in them than a few scant references does justice to. Just as *Evil Dead II* exhibits all the hallmarks of the neo-baroque – that is, an accumulative and largely chaotic abundance of signifiers that point not to one source but to an infinite network of (inter)textual bases – then *Re-Animator* too, in its utilisation of various contexts for horror (monsters, comedy, gore, etc.), demonstrates how multifarious and multifaceted textual antecedents operate beneath the surface. In its citation of, homage to, and send-up of the classic monster text, namely *Frankenstein*, *Re-Animator* illustrates the acuity of Ndalianis's observations.

What emerges out of a broader consideration of the complex network of signifiers, both manifest and latent, that contribute to a text's primary features, is recognition that influence is not a simple thing but is in fact dependent on a variety of textual, cultural and industrial factors. Sean Cubitt's work on the supernatural in modern Hollywood filmmaking offers a compelling take on the subject of the neo-baroque. He states that:

> Neo-baroque space offers itself for the immersion of the spectator in the spectacle [...] The immersion is itself an allegory [...] of a satisfaction that comes from bathing in the apogee of consumerism. (2009: 52)

Reading films such as *Evil Dead II* and *Re-Animator* within the critical framework offered by the neo-baroque, it is clear to see how film's past emerges as an inhabitable space to be occupied by later texts.[34] The effect is accumulative and largely operates beyond concrete qualification. If one considers, for example, the critical and commercial popularity of preceding horror-comedies such as *Ghostbusters* and *Gremlins* as sources of influence, then one will see how intertextual heritage manifests in a range of ways across different eras of productions and various generic and subgeneric formations.

It is clear in the time since *Re-Animator* that the taste for mad science horror has never truly disappeared, at least not in the way that Tudor forecast. From the mid-1980s to present there has been a range of variably successful mad science horror films both with and without cult appeal. These films include, but are not limited to, *The Fly*, *From Beyond*, *Prince of Darkness* (John Carpenter, 1987), *Hellraiser II: Hellbound* (Tony Randall, 1988), *Bride of Re-Animator*, *The Fly II* (Chris Walas, 1989), the *Tetsuo* series (Shinya Tsukamoto, 1989-2009), *Hardware* (Richard Stanley, 1990), *Flatliners* (Joel Schumacher, 1991), *The Lawnmower Man* (Brett Leonard, 1992), *Jurassic Park* (Steven Spielberg, 1993), *Death Machine* (Stephen Norrington, 1995), *eXistenZ* (David Cronenberg, 1999), *Hollow Man* (Paul Verhoeven, 2000), *Jason X* (Jim Isaac, 2001), *28 Days Later* (Danny Boyle, 2002), the *Resident Evil* series (Paul W. S. Anderson, 2002-16), *Beyond Re-Animator*,

Sunshine (Danny Boyle, 2007), the *Cloverfield* series (various, 2008–present), the *Outpost* series (various, 2008-13), *Splice* (Vincenzo Natali, 2009), *American Mary* (Jen and Sylvia Soska, 2012), *Alien* prequels *Prometheus* and *Alien: Covenant* (Ridley Scott, 2012; 2017), *Frankenstein's Army* (Richard Raaphorst, 2013), *Ex Machina* (Alex Garland, 2014), *Victor Frankenstein* (Paul McGuigan, 2015), *Get Out* (Jordan Peele, 2017), *Overlord* (Julius Avery, 2018), *Upgrade* (Leigh Whannell, 2018) and *Rabid* (Jen and Sylvia Soska, 2019).[35] While it is clear that these films exhibit a range of broader influences, inviting consideration of the ways in which corresponding subgenres overlap and interlock within the larger pantheon of horror films, they nevertheless all in some way illustrate the mad science subgenre, which was restored, in part, by *Re-Animator*'s initial success and enduring popularity.

Footnotes

21. See Thomas Schatz, "The Studio System and Contemporary Hollywood" (2008: 13-42).
22. See Schatz 2008, above, as well as Stephen Prince's volume *A New Pot of Gold: Hollywood Under the Electronic Rainbow, 1980-89* (1999).
23. See also, Jason Zinoman's similarly oriented book *Shock Value: How a Few Eccentric Outsiders Gave Us Nightmares, Conquered Hollywood, and Invented Modern Horror* (2011).
24. A subject I explore at greater length in chapter one.
25. All data has been collected from *the-numbers* and *BoxOfficeMojo* (accessed May 2019).
26. Channeling definitions of blockbusters from Justin Wyatt (1994) and Richard Maltby (1998: 21-44), Stacey Abbott traces the shifting industrial context for horror blockbusters from 1990s-present (2010: 27-45).
27. I have included, as an appendix to this volume, an interview I conducted with *Fangoria*'s current editor Phil Nobile Jr. in which we discuss *Re-Animator* and the 1980s horror scene.
28. For an overview, see Vera Dika, *Games of Terror: Halloween, Friday the 13th, and the Films of the Stalker Cycle* (1990).
29. *Gremlins*'s status as a family horror film was the subject of much controversy at the time of its release (see Zoglin 1984: n.p.). Indeed, alongside *Indiana Jones and the Temple of Doom* (Steven Spielberg, 1984), the release of *Gremlins* as a PG certificate prompted the re-evaluation of the US ratings systems which led to the creation of the PG-13 rating. For more on the topic of 1980s American horror films that traversed the child / adult boundary, see Catherine Lester, *Horror Films for Children: Fear and Pleasure in American Cinema* (2021).
30. Discussed in Aldana Reyes (2014: 52-73).

31. Following Wes Craven's horror output of the mid-1990s — see, for example, *Wes Craven's New Nightmare* (1994) and *Scream* (1996) — one might notice a rise in what might be called meta-horror films, including *Shaun of the Dead* (Edgar Wright, 2004), *Zombieland* (Reuben Fleischer, 2009), *Tucker & Dale Vs. Evil* (Eli Craig, 2010), and *The Cabin in the Woods* (Drew Goddard, 2012).
32. See also, Meredith Brody, "We Killed 'Em in Chicago" (1987: 74).
33. For an example of discourse that was celebrating SFX artists as auteurs, see *Fangoria*'s cover story on Tom Savini in *Fangoria* #27 (1983).
34. See Brooks's *Young Frankenstein* for perhaps the clearest of examples.
35. I would contend that many comic books films utilise the mad science trope as the source of their villains' exploits. I would further argue that these are rooted in the themes and iconography of horror even if the films, in general, cannot be aligned with the genre. See, for example: *Spider-Man 2* (Sam Raimi, 2004), *Captain America: The First Avenger* (Joe Johnston, 2011) and *Wonder Woman* (Patty Jenkins, 2017).

Chapter Four: "I gave him life!" *Re-Animator*, Stuart Gordon and the Birth of a New Lovecraftian Cycle

Examining Lovecraftian Adaptations

> No writer, not even his great predecessor Edgar Allan Poe, conjoins popular and critical renown in this manner – S.T. Joshi (2013: xv)

As I stipulated in the previous chapter, Stuart Gordon's *Re-Animator* is not only a fascinating film that brings together horror's literary past with the genre's filmic present, but also represents the beginning of both a new cycle of Lovecraft films and a directing career that was largely indebted to that particular author's work. As such, as fascinating as *Re-Animator*'s placement within 1980s horror is, equally compelling is its relatively privileged position within the larger history of Lovecraft in adaptation.

So who exactly was H.P. Lovecraft? With the exception of Stephen King, H.P. (Howard Philips) Lovecraft is arguably the most famous writer of twentieth-century American horror. In his short lifetime,[36] Lovecraft was plagued by various troubles financial, personal and health-related. Indeed, he found little success with his writing, and died in sad circumstances, in poor health and virtual anonymity. In the years following his death, however, Lovecraft gained a substantial reputation for his weird tales of cosmic horror that included short stories such as "The Color Out of Space" (1927), "The Call of Cthulhu" (1928) and "The Dunwich Horror" (1929), novellas including *At the Mountains of Madness* (1936) and *The Shadow Over Innsmouth* (1936), and even a full novel, *The Case of Charles Dexter Ward* (published posthumously in 1941). Today, the Cthulhu mythos that ties together many of his works is the basis of a transmedial phenomenon that incorporates everything from a multitude of fiction and film adaptations to role-playing games and so forth. Recently, cult director Richard Stanley joined forces with sometimes-cult star Nicholas Cage for the Lovecraft adaption *Color Out of Space* (2019), while HBO's subsequent tentpole release of *Lovecraft Country* in 2020 brings the author's mythos to life once again in a work that reveres his imagination while rightly aspiring to challenge his ghastly ideas about race.

Lovecraft obsessive S.T. Joshi has largely been responsible for both reviving interest in, and developing a scholarly appreciation of, the works of Lovecraft, and has been at the centre of a growing field of study focussed on his oeuvre. Joshi has written copious volumes on Lovecraft, including an expansive biography (1996), as well as articles, introductions, editorials and so forth, and has collected and overseen the publication of almost everything Lovecraft related, from fiction and poetry to letters and essays. These materials have been arranged and released with the intention of raising Lovecraft from his pulp origins and cementing his status as one of the most enduring American writers of the modernist period. Few would argue with the assertion that Joshi remains the most dedicated Lovecraft scholar working today. Indeed, after years of work by Joshi and others, the time has come in which the need "for defending Lovecraft as a genuine literary figure is long past [for] his ascent to the canon of American and world literature is now complete" (Joshi 2013: xv).

The deep philosophical trajectories of Lovecraft's work have been been mined by various writers, including Maurice Lévy who writes of both the micro- and macro-cosmic elements of his thematic corpus:

> It was precisely Lovecraft's merit to discover, beyond the historical data of his own country, the structure of the great myths that have nourished humanity. In *dreaming* the past of New England, the home of sorcerers, he recommenced an archaic tradition, transcending local peculiarities. The strange, the disquieting, the abnormal emerge from this surfacing of the primordial into the contemporary. America, too, can become a fantastic world, because it was from Salem that Lovecraft recreated the Cosmos. (1988: 16)

Here, Lévy alludes to the near-mythic reverence of Lovecraft's work which is no doubt indebted to the allure of his "strange […] disquieting […] abnormal" visions of the universe's horrific machinations. It is clear from the surfeit of adaptations across various media that Lovecraft remains, to this day, one of the great literary and philosophical influencers of early twentieth-century American literature.

Lovecraft's gradual suffusion into the wider landscape of popular culture has had various elemental parts. Joshi writes of Lovecraft's belated popularity in print, noting that collected volumes of his short stories found great success by the late 1960s and soon began to inspire critical inquiries that culminated with his own work from the early 1980s onwards. Since the release of Roger Corman's *The Haunted Palace* in 1963 — a film that was wrongly marketed as a Poe adaptation in order to coincide with a popular series of adaptations starring Vincent Price, but was in fact an adaptation of *The Case of Charles Dexter Ward* — there has been a steady flow of feature adaptations of Lovecraft's work. Indeed, in Stephen Follows's 2017 *Horror Report*, the author finds Lovecraft to be the fourth most adapted horror author after Poe, Stevenson and Stoker (2017: 25). Migliore and Stryslik have intimated towards Lovecraft's transcultural and transmedial presence in their introduction to a survey of screen adaptations of his work:

> As sure as Cthulhu waits dreaming, short films, theatrical features, television shows, and children's cartoons, with budgets big and small, will continue to be adapted from—and inspired by—the works of this eternally fascinating writer who gleefully plagued the early twentieth century with cosmic horror too terrible to describe. (2006: 4)

Indeed, much has been made of Lovecraft's unending influence on film. From direct adaptations such as *Re-Animator* to films bearing the author's DNA, if not his actual name — including Ridley Scott's *Alien* and John Carpenter's *The Thing* — Lovecraft's cosmic weirdness has come to have a distinct role in the iconographic development of the horror genre on film. To place into context the different types of Lovecraft films, and periods of interest in his works, I have constructed a table to offer details on some of the major works of adaptation.[37]

Year	Film / director	Based on	Notes
1963	*The Haunted Palace* (Roger Corman)	*The Case of Charles Dexter Ward* (1941)	Wrongly advertised as a Poe adaptation to coincide with the popularity of the Corman/Price series in the early 1960s.
1965	*Die, Monster, Die!* (Daniel Haller)	"The Color Out of Space" (1927)	A British-American collaboration that was distributed by Roger Corman's American International Pictures (AIP).
1968	*The Crimson Cult* (Vernon Sewell)	"The Dreams in the Witch House" (1933)	An uncredited adaptation.
1970	*The Dunwich Horror* (Daniel Haller)	"The Dunwich Horror" (1929)	The first feature to be released under one of Lovecraft's original titles.

1985	*Re-Animator* (Stuart Gordon)	"Herbert West—Re-Animator" (1922)	*Re-Animator* marked a return to Lovecraft adaptations after a 15 year hiatus following *The Dunwich Horror*. Its success initiated a cycle of adaptations to be released over the next decade or so.
1986	*From Beyond* (Stuart Gordon)	"From Beyond" (1934)	A return to Lovecraft for many of the cast and crew of *Re-Animator*.
1987	*The Curse* (David Keith)	"The Color Out of Space" (1927)	A small B-movie that has since found cult appreciation on home release.
1988	*The Unnamable* (Jean-Paul Ouellette)	"The Unnamable" (1925)	Distributed by Vidmark Entertainment, a subsidiary of Trimark Pictures who would later support some of *Re-Animator* producer Brian Yuzna's directorial work.
1990	*Bride of Re-Animator* (Brian Yuzna)	"Herbert West—Re-Animator" (1922)	The first sequel to Gordon's film that riffs heavily on *Bride of Frankenstein*
1992	*The Resurrected* (Dan O'Bannon)	*The Case of Charles Dexter Ward* (1941)	O'Bannon, famous for *The Return of the Living Dead* would go on to be screenwriter for another Lovecraft adaptation, *Bleeders*.
1993	*Necronomicon* (Brian Yuzna, Christophe Gans and Shusuke Kaneko)	"The Rats in the Walls" (1924), "Cool Air" (1928), and *The Whisperer in Darkness* (1931)	An anthology film based on three Lovecraft stories.
	The Unnamable 2: The Statement of Randolph Carter (Jean-Paul Ouellette)	"The Statement of Randolph Carter" (1920)	A sequel to *The Unnamable*.
1994	*The Lurking Fear* (C. Courtney Joyner)	"The Lurking Fear" (1923)	Produced by Full Moon Features, the company Charles Band started following the collapse of EIP.
1995	*Castle Freak* (Stuart Gordon)	"The Outsider" (1926)	Another Full Moon Features production.
1997	*Bleeders* (Peter Svatek)	"The Lurking Fear" (1923)	Also released under the title *Hemoglobin* in certain territories.

1999	Cool Air (Bryan Moore)	"Cool Air" (1928)	Part of The H. P. Lovecraft Collection, a series of independent films selected from submissions to the Lovecraft Film Festival.
2001	Dagon (Stuart Gordon)	The Shadow Over Innsmouth (1936)	The title is a misnomer as the film has only a passing resemblance to "Dagon" (1919) and more closely follows the plot of The Shadow Over Innsmouth. The film was produced by Yuzna's company Fantastic Factory who would go on to produce Beyond Re-Animator.
2003	Beyond Re-Animator (Brian Yuzna)	"Herbert West - Re-Animator" (1922)	The second sequel to Gordon's film.
2005	Dreams in the Witch House (Stuart Gordon)	"The Dreams in the Witch House" (1933)	Part of Mick Garris's Master of Horror anthology series (2005-7). Gordon's other contribution was The Black Cat (2007) in Season two, a Poe adaptation.
	The Call of Cthulhu (Andrew Leman)	"The Call of Cthulhu" (1928)	A silent, black and white adaptation distributed by the H. P. Lovecraft Historical Society.
2006	Beyond the Wall of Sleep (Barrett J. Leigh and Thom Maurer)	"Beyond the Wall of Sleep" (1919)	A very low-budget production.
2007	Cthulhu (Daniel Gildark)	The Shadow Over Innsmouth (1936)	This film, like Dagon above, has a misleading title that suggests it is based on "The Call of Cthulhu", not The Shadow Over Innsmouth.
2011	The Whisperer in Darkness (Sean Branney)	The Whisperer in Darkness (1931)	An independent production that resembles the vintage aesthetic of The Call of Cthulhu (2005). Notably, it was also distributed by the H. P. Lovecraft Historical Society.
2013	Banshee Chapter (Blair Erickson)	"From Beyond" (1934)	Stars Ted Levine, famous for playing Buffalo Bill in The Silence of the Lambs (Jonathan Demme, 1991).

2016	*Howard Lovecraft and the Frozen Kingdom* (Sean Patrick O'Reilly)	Various stories concerning the characters and events of the Cthulhu mythos.	A family-oriented re-telling of various stories by Lovecraft. Inspired two sequels in 2017 and 2019.
2019	*Color Out of Space* (Richard Stanley)	*The Color Out of Space* (1927)	This adaptation of *The Color Out of Space* marked the return of cult director Richard Stanley (*Hardware*, *Dust Devil* [1993]), directing his first feature since leaving production of *The Island of Dr Moreau* (John Frankenheimer, 1996).

Table 4.1 – A survey of Lovecraft film adaptations from 1963-present

What is clear from a survey of Lovecraft in adaptation is that films based on his works have largely circumvented what might be considered the mainstream of the horror genre. Mark Jones writes as much, stating that "Lovecraftian horror retains its cultish trappings and appeal" (2013: 227-8), placing its primary fandom at the fringe of horror film fans. Coinciding with the fact that at the time of writing Guillermo del Toro's long-gestating adaption of *At The Mountains of Madness* is still no closer to being green-lit for production,[38] it is notable that there have been relatively few Lovecraft adaptations to come out of major studios.[39] Furthermore, with the exception of *Re-Animator*, few of the productions listed above have had much in the way of success, at least not beyond cultist collecting tendencies attributed to horror films of the VHS era.[40]

While scholars have written of the general lack of quality in Lovecraft film adaptations (Jones 2018), elsewhere critics have found that film versions of Lovecraft have had a profound impact on a wider appreciation of the author's work. John Wisdom Gonce, for example, writes that "the interwoven concepts of Lovecraft's fiction, the *Necronomicon* legend, and the nature of magickal practices have all been defined in the public imagination by the reality-shaping propaganda/entertainment industry of film" (2003: 225). As overwrought as his analysis of the medium of film as a "reality-shaping propaganda" machine may be, Gonce's words nevertheless do make the compelling point that adaptations of Lovecraft have an overriding authority in the wider understanding and adoption of both his works and the ideas contained within them. Negative criticism for Lovecraft adaptations has been levelled by multitudinous censurers affronted by the broader corpus of 1980s horror, which has been dismissed in turn by critics, scholars and audiences as being superficial and daft at best and vicious and exploitative at worst. It is nevertheless interesting to note Gonce's inference, that things do get lost in translation when textual specifics are transported between vastly different mediums. It is fair to argue that *Re-Animator* loses some of the philosophical substance of Lovecraft, however other works, especially HBO's recent series *Lovecraft Country*, have actively sought to transform the source material, seen in the show's attempt to recast the despicable racism that lurks at the heart of Lovecraft's work in order to explore sources of real-world monstrosity that continue to plague the nation, namely the ever-present threat of white supremacism.

Re-Animator was largely championed by critics as one of the better screen adaptations of a Lovecraft story, yet it remains vastly different to its source, to the extent that writers have argued that, for all its qualities, it is far from what one might call "Lovecraftian" in the philosophical sense. Indeed, there has been a steady flow of debate about the quality and direction of screen adaptations of Lovecraft. Consolidating such debates, Steffen Hantke writes:

> Though there is disagreement whether Lovecraft's work has of yet produced a great adaptation on the screen or not — a debate akin to that among academics about the relative degree of his canonical centrality — there is both a list of contenders, as well as a sense that, even without a single outstanding adaptation, Lovecraft's influence throughout twentieth- and twenty-first-century horror film has been pervasive. (2013: 136)

Despite Hantke's keenness to lay claim to Lovecraft's influence on film screen cultures – he writes later of "countless unacknowledged visual and conceptual references to Lovecraft's mythological history and pantheon in films otherwise unconnected to his name" (136) – he is reticent to commit to the idea that a film adaptation has truly done Lovecraft's work justice, though he does, significantly, underline *Re-Animator* as one of the outstanding "contenders".

Lovecraft's epistemological obsession with matters out of reach, the horrors of the unknowable and "unnameable", to invoke the title of his 1925 short story, has arguably been a source of insurmountable difficulty for adapters of his work. From a practical filmmaking perspective, as well as from a more cogently cognitive one, Jones notes that

"Lovecraft's massive and indifferent creatures, operating on an utterly dissimilar scale to human life and values, are more difficult to portray or narrativize" (2013: 231). Offering support of Hantke's claim for Lovecraft's enduring influence on films that are not direct adaptations, Murray Leeder similarly identifies Lovecraftian elements in David Robert Mitchell's *It Follows* (2014), observing that the film captures aspects of the author's philosophical outlook as "a pessimist deeply concerned with epistemology – what can be known, and especially what lies beyond knowledge" (2019: 11).

Thematically speaking, for Matthew Green in his analysis of graphic novelist Alan Moore's excursions into Lovecraft,[41] Lovecraft's writing details "[violent] forces capable not only of violating bodies, but of bursting through the very fabric of time and space" (2013: 254). Matching that description, Joshi writes, "Lovecraft's philosophical position virtually necessitated the central conception in his aesthetic of the weird — the notion of cosmicism, or the suggestion of vast gulfs of space and time and the resultant inconsequence of the human species" (2011: xvii). It is fair to say that adapters have often struggled to capture Lovecraft's cosmicism, which operates on a metaphysical level that genre filmmakers often struggle to reach.[42] I would argue, in fact, that Gordon's second Lovecraft film, *From Beyond*, comes closer to what has traditionally been understood as Lovecraftian, especially in reference to the author's profound and arresting cosmicism. Indeed, what *Re-Animator* gains by way of tongue-in-cheek intertextuality and gore by the gallon comes at the cost of truly capturing the nihilistic ineffability of Lovecraft's worldview. Lovecraftian horror goes beyond the material facts of the world to scrutinise the "fabric" of things at a cosmically macroscopic level. But that is not to say that *Re-Animator* does not try.

Re-Animator as Adaptation

So how does one approach *Re-Animator* as an adaptation of Lovecraft? As this book has hopefully demonstrated, the film's qualities and points of interest are plentiful, but how does it figure in relation to the textual and thematic substance of work it is based upon? As Linda Hutcheon has written, an adaptation grants a text a new life: "an adaptation, like the work it adapts, is always framed in a context – a time and a place, a society and a culture; it does not exist in a vacuum" (2006: 142). Rather than relate, at length, the plot elements of Lovecraft's short story, "Herbert West – Re-Animator", which is told episodically over a series of short accounts by a nameless narrator (Cain in the film), I will instead focus on ways in which Gordon's film captures the "spirit" of Lovecraft, as well as the transcultural utility of his oeuvre.

For Joshi, key to Lovecraftian cosmicism is a profound fear of the unknown that forever stalks the edge of what is known. This epistemological discordance that is fundamental to Lovecraft is expressed early on in "Herbert West – Re-Animator", as the narrator begins to recount his tale:

> Now that [West] is gone and the spell is broken, the actual fear is greater. Memories and possibilities are ever more hideous than realities. (Lovecraft 2011 [1922]: 50)

Across the breadth of his fiction, Lovecraft shows a recurring preoccupation with the inexplicable, so much so that the unspeakable sights that his characters encounter are often only intimated towards and not described plainly. While a cynic might mark such descriptive omissions as a failure of imagination, for many they are a key source of intrigue that offer a platform for new epistemological and eschatological byroads. In screen adaptations, of course, the extradimensional elements of Lovecraft's fictive realms are less speculative and operate within more concretely realised terms. As the murky depths of Lovecraft's imagination materialise, the forms become less frightening for the simple fact that, rendered through a primarily visual medium, the shapeless is given shape. In other words, in screen adaptations the inexpressible is bound to be expressed and, by virtue of that expression, the cataclysmic horror of Lovecraftian cosmicism falls away or collapses entirely. *Re-Animator* arguably comes closest to Lovecraftian cosmicism in its finale where Hill mutates into a gory abomination that drags West away to an unfathomable beyond, in a sequence that Worland refers to as the pinnacle of the film's "absurdist dance of gore and burlesque" (2006: 251).[43] Even in this sequence, which comes tantalisingly close to invoking the cosmic extradimensional horror of Lovecraft's prose, Worland underscores it as markedly visual; so as much as the sequence is a fun and gory spectacle, this apotheotic denouement does little to shift the film away from its roots as a prototypical zombie narrative.

Some characteristics of Gordon's adaptation critically engage with problems that are inherent to Lovecraft's story (and to his writing in general). First, there is the creation of

Megan, who is wholly absent from Lovecraft's short story – in fact, there are virtually no female characters in the original text. As well as addressing the sexlessness of Lovecraft's prose, the creation of Megan serves *Re-Animator*'s commercial viability on the back of the success of the slasher subgenre which, as I detailed in the previous chapter, was a popular if waning mode at the time of the film's development. Second, Gordon's adaptation removes much of the overt racism of Lovecraft's original text. In one episode in particular, West and his accomplice find themselves with an African-American subject that the narrator unspeakably describes as a "loathsome, gorilla-like thing […] that conjured up thoughts of unspeakable Congo secrets and tom-tom poundings under an eerie moon" (63). It will be unsurprising to a modern reader that such elements have been removed from the story, but these are elements that are strongly iterative of prejudices that recur throughout Lovecraft's work and which offer insight into a worldview that is hampered by supremacist logic and racial bias. Indeed, Lovecraft's derisive racism has prompted modern readers and critics to reevaluate his status, which led to his removal from the bust of the World Fantasy Award trophy as of 2015 and to revisionist adaptations of his work such as *Lovecraft Country*.

Different too is Jeffrey Combs's characterisation of West. While West is just as arch and dogged in his determination as his filmic counterpart, Lovecraft's story lacks the humour that is central to Combs's performance. Consider the narrator's description of West's ethos and ambition in the Lovecraft story:

> That the tradition-bound elders should ignore his singular results on animals, and persist in their denial of the possibility of reanimation, was inexpressibly disgusting and almost incomprehensible to a youth of West's logical temperament. Only greater maturity could help him understand the chronic mental limitations of the "professor-doctor" type – the product of generations of pathetic Puritanism; kindly, conscientious, and sometimes gentle and amiable, yet always narrow, intolerant, custom-ridden, and lacking in perspective. Age has more charity for these incomplete yet high-souled characters, whose worst real vice is timidity, and who are ultimately punished by general ridicule for their intellectual sins – sins like Ptolemaism, Calvinism, anti-Darwinism, anti-Nietzscheism, and every sort of Sabbatarianism and sumptuary legislation. West, young despite his marvellous scientific acquirements, had scant patience with good Dr. Halsey and his erudite colleagues; and nursed an increasing

resentment, coupled with a desire to prove his theories to these obtuse worthies in some striking and dramatic fashion. (56-7)

As I outlined in chapter three, there are a number of sequences in *Re-Animator* that demonstrate the film's prominence among horror-comedies, but it is worth underlining the fact that much of its humour relies on Jeffrey Combs's performance. All in all, Combs's West is more than an anachronistic revival of a mad scientist in the tradition of *Frankenstein*; his West is an explosion of intertextual and performed elements that combine to deliver the character's cult appeal. The extract above outlines the philosophical basis for West's anomalous regard for his human subjects; Lovecraft's West is guided by scientific discovery above all else, and his ruthlessness in the pursuit of his aims leads him down murderous pathways. In the film, however, Combs leans into West's eccentricity, utilising the character's wholly different ethical construction of the world as the basis for zany, character-driven humour. Indeed, in his assessment of the film, Worland notes how Combs's characterisation of West as an over-the-top, pantomimic anti-hero brings levity to sequences that might otherwise induce more volatile reactions in their audience (2006: 243-252). For example, in his execution of Hill — which he does by decapitating him with the hard edge of a shovel — West emphatically declares him to be a "plagiarist" as he delivers his lethal blow, delivered in such a manner as to suggest that it is intellectual rivalry that has spurred him towards violence, and not merely the matter of self-defence.

It is interesting to see how some aspects of Lovecraft's original story that are absent in Gordon's adaptation have been employed in other ways later. A war-set episode in Lovecraft's story, for instance, finds its way (though transposed from one war to another) into the film's sequel, *Bride of Re-Animator*, which opens during the Peruvian civil war. In both the Lovecraft story and the introduction of *Bride of Re-Animator*, the episode finds West experimenting with dismembered body parts, and is intended as further evidence of his ruthlessness: "all this research work required a prodigious supply of freshly slaughtered human flesh – and that was why Herbert West had entered the Great War" (73). There is clearly nothing noble in West's call to arms and, while it would not have worked in the narrative of Gordon's original film, it is nevertheless a striking sequence, which explains its adoption for the sequel. It is interesting that, in its finale, *Bride of Re-Animator* once again borrows from Lovecraft's story with a climax that takes place in the tombs adjacent to his laboratory, a scene which recalls 'The Tomb-Legions' in the text (a lengthier discussion of *Bride of Re-Animator* will follow in the final chapter).

Overall, what Gordon's film demonstrates is how a literary source can be employed for a drastically different context while retaining elements of the original text. What one sees in Gordon's *Re-Animator* is a reworking of the material to suit the context of the film's production in the aftermath of the 1980s slasher boom. Such "reworkings" have been theorised by adaptation scholar Robert Stam as what he calls the "dialogics of adaptation". Stam writes:

> One way to look at adaptation is to see it as a complex series of operations: selection, amplification, concretization, actualization, critique, extrapolation, analogization, popularization, and reculturalization. The source novel, in this sense, can be seen as a situated utterance produced in one medium and in one historical context, then transformed into another equally situated utterance that is produced in a different context and in a different medium. (2000: 68)

In line with this conceptualisation, Gordon's adaptation may be construed as the sort of newly "situated utterance" of Lovecraft's story that Stam describes, one that conveys a series of particulars that root it in the midst of 1980s horror filmmaking. Gordon's film demonstrates the adaptive qualities of Lovecraft's work, and punctuates his sustained cultural significance as a twentieth-century horror author, while simultaneously situating the story within a new, intertextual (and, later, intermedial) network of works which collectively foster new meaning and modes of authorship.[44] Therefore, as important as it is to consider *Re-Animator* as an adaptation of Lovecraft, it is equally important – especially in the context of his ongoing project to adapt Lovecraft – to look at Gordon as an adapter with his own authorial prerogatives.

LOVECRAFTIAN ADAPTATION IN THE FILMS OF STUART GORDON

Returning to a case I made in chapter one, it is fair to argue that *Re-Animator* is about as strong a film as Charles Band's Empire International Pictures ever did make. It is also reasonable, I would suggest, to propose that Stuart Gordon was the best technical filmmaker working within the studio at any time during its run. Indeed, Linda Badley has argued for Gordon's status as a "horror auteur", by which she is referring to "the large number of notable recent directors whose films are recognized as employing, throughout a body of work, horror film syntax and themes to express, often self-reflexively and 'subversively,' their 'visions'" (2004: 224-5). Listing Gordon beside other notable horror auteurs including Dario Argento, Clive Barker, Mario Bava, Tim Burton, John Carpenter, Wes Craven, David Cronenberg, Larry Cohen, Brian De Palma, Abel Ferrara, Lucio Fulci, Tobe Hooper, David Lynch, Roman Polanski, Sam Raimi, Jean Rollin, George Romero and Ken Russell, Badley makes a case for, firstly, unstitching any existing critical distinctions between "high" and "low" forms of horror (ie. Polanski's highbrow literariness beside Rollin's sex-fuelled exploitation films), as well as a case for marking Gordon out as a filmmaker with an overriding "vision" to speak of.

This vision is well worth scrutinising in the context of Gordon's ongoing interest in the works of Lovecraft, represented by adaptations over a twenty-year period: *From Beyond*, *Castle Freak*, *Dagon* and *Dreams in the Witch House*, a TV movie that featured as part of Mick Garris's *Masters of Horror* series (2005-7), a series that was for some critics important for determining auteur status among contemporary horror filmmakers.[45] Joe Hickinbottom, in a chapter on Takashi Miike's horror reputation, makes use of Garris's *Masters of Horror* as a prism through which to observe the discursive and economic functions of the horror auteur, and how such statuses are conferred and capitalised upon. Hickinbottom writes that "*Masters of Horror* was accordingly billed as an opportunity for audiences to indulge in the nightmarish work of some of horror cinema's greatest directors" (2020: 95). While Gordon's status as a horror master is less contentious than, say, Miike's,[46] it nevertheless invigorates a way of looking at the director's work that invites one to situate it within the principle tenets of auteurism.

Joe Tompkins has identified how important the idea of the auteur is to the marketing of horror. In his assessment of horror auteurism and the splat pack — referring to a group of popular "torture porn" filmmakers such as Eli Roth, James Wan and Rob Zombie who all emerged in the early twenty-first century — Tompkins claims the following:

> [A]uteurism remains central to the marketing of some horror films. The invocation of horror auteurs has tended to permit critics, fans, and filmmakers to accumulate subcultural capital by expressing their appreciation of, and affiliation with, ultraviolent

horror. What is more, this practice has become part of industry practice, with production and distribution personnel seeking to invest themselves and their output with the subcultural authenticity that is associated with a cohort of 1970s horror directors. (2014: 212)

For Tompkins, there is a transgenerational correspondence at work between auteurs of the past such as Argento, Craven and Carpenter and the emerging horror directors of the mid-2000s. Furthermore, for Tompkins, the conferment of the status of "horror auteur" has a discursive utility, and tells audiences something about the nature of a filmmaker's output; the assignment delineates a working prolificacy, a thematic cohesion between works, an economic incentive on the part of distributors and a demand to take the work seriously. Gordon falls through the cracks of Tompkins's work, which largely looks at the discursive function of the auteur tag in the 1970s and mid-2000s, however it is clear that for some (including Badley, 2010), Gordon's work has the same auteurist elements of earlier horror filmmakers.

In terms of thematic cohesion across works, *From Beyond*, Gordon and Yuzna's second collaboration for EIP, follows the *Re-Animator* template quite carefully. Disregarding for a moment Gordon's later career, based on just these two films it would be fair to make claims that Gordon was already developing a taste for horror (and, indeed, Lovecraft) that was markedly auterist. There is a moment early on in *From Beyond* which feels like a reflexive acknowledgement of that fact. The scene in question involves a disgruntled neighbour complaining to the police about the disturbing experiments taking place next door: "they're at it again", she tells the authorities in disbelief. Of course, in the context of the film, the neighbour is principally referring to the diabolical experiments of Dr. Edward Pretorius (Ted Sorel) and his assistant Dr. Crawford Tillinghast (played by Jeffrey Combs). One might equally suspect that her accusation has a second, extratextual function, that it is also a nod in the direction of Gordon and Yuzna to mark the duo's return to their Lovecraftian playground.

From Beyond is as close as one might imagine to a by-the-numbers reconfiguration of everything that worked so well in *Re-Animator*. The film features both returning crew members, including Gordon, producer Yuzna, writer Dennis Paoli, editor Lee Percy, cinematographer Mac Ahlberg and composer Richard Band, and returning performers,

Fig. 4.1 – Jeffrey Combs and Barbara Crampton return for From Beyond *(dir. Stuart Gordon, 1986).*

including lead stars Combs and Barbara Crampton, as well as members of the supporting cast such as Carolyn Purdy-Gordon and Bunny Summers. Furthermore, *From Beyond*'s plot is not far removed from *Re-Animator*'s either. *From Beyond* opens *in media res* with two scientists' attempt to access adjacent dimensions using a device called a resonator that works by stimulating the participant's pineal gland. In the Lovecraftian tradition, their experiment goes badly wrong, creating a gateway to another realm through which creatures appear to drag Pretorius to what lies beyond. Facing a possible murder charge due to the disappearance of his accomplice, Tillinghast is left no choice but to return to the scene of the accident and repeat the experiment under the supervision of an ambitious doctor (Barbara Crampton) and a macho detective (Ken Foree). Combs and Crampton get to have fun in inverted roles – Combs, here, as the traumatised "scream queen" of sorts, and Crampton as the deranged scientist hell-bent on the possibility of new discoveries. The film maintains similarities with *Re-Animator* at its thematic core, with the motif of male bravado concealing sexual impotence making a return in the character of Pretorius who sexually assaults Crampton's Dr. Katherine McMichaels in a scene that brings to mind Hill's assault of Megan in the earlier film. The finale finds Tillinghast faced off against Pretorius, who has returned as a grotesque interdimensional monstrosity that resembles the abomination that Hill becomes in *Re-Animator*.

In an interview with John Andrew Gallagher, Gordon admits that he "really like[s] the idea of doing a series of Lovecraft movies that have an ensemble company in them, sort of like the old Roger Corman Poe movies with Vincent Price. Jeffrey Combs is my Vincent Price" (qtd in Gallagher 1989: 98). There is a sense from this quotation that, as early as the late-1980s, Gordon already imagined himself as a horror auteur of sorts, albeit one that was aligned more with Corman's B-movie credentials as opposed to some other, loftier horror filmmakers. As it happened, there were many detours between Gordon making *From Beyond* in 1986 and his next Lovecraft adaptation, *Castle Freak*, in 1995, almost a decade later. In the interim, Gordon took a stab at Poe with a remake of *The Pit and the Pendulum* (originally part of the Corman-Price-Poe cycle aforementioned), while Yuzna branched off to direct some of his own films, including *Bride of Re-Animator* in 1990. By the time Gordon and writer Dennis Paoli returned to Lovecraft with a take on another (this time very) short story, "The Outsider" (1926), there had been an assortment of Lovecraft films released, including *The Unnamable*, *The Resurrected*, *Necronomicon* and *The Lurking Fear*, a project that Gordon himself had previously been considering.

Castle Freak plays out quite differently to *Re-Animator* and *From Beyond*. The film once again features Gordon favourites Combs and Crampton, this time as John and Susan Reilly, an estranged married couple dealing with the recent loss of their son, for which John is responsible. The couple are travelling to Italy with their teenage daughter, blinded from the same drink driving accident that killed their son, in order to inspect a castle that John has inherited from a (seemingly) distant relative, who served as Duchess at the castle. It soon becomes clear that the duchess's monstrous son, Giorgio, long thought dead, continues to live in the depths of the castle, and is now bloodthirsty after years of imprisonment and torture at the hands of his deranged, lovesick mother. It turns out that the duchess is also John's mother and therefore Giorgio is his brother. In the final act, John sacrifices himself to save his family from Giorgio; as he dies, Susan forgives him for his sins. With a budget of around half a million dollars, *Castle Freak* was reportedly the cheapest film that Gordon ever made. In 1995, it was a direct-to-video release for Full Moon Features, but has since found cult appreciation with special feature-laden releases on various horror series, including collectible editions from 88 Films (UK), Wizard Entertainment (USA) and Wicked-Vision Media (Germany).

Brian Yuzna returned to production duties on *Dagon* in 2001, following his absence from *Castle Freak*. *Dagon* was one of a handful of films produced by Fantastic Factory, a small production company specialising in low-budget horror and science-fiction that was created by Yuzna and Julio Fernández as a subsidiary of Filmax. Bookended by two films directed by Yuzna himself, *Faust: Love of the Damned* in 2000 and *Beneath Still Waters* in 2006, Fantastic Factory had only a small amount of success. Indeed, *Dagon* and *Beyond Re-Animator* have achieved the most in the way of cult status over the years, a matter marked by back-to-back prestige re-releases in a collector's series by US home distributor Vestron Video in 2018.[47] Despite a misleading title, *Dagon* is in fact mostly based on *The Shadow Over Innsmouth*. Following an incident at sea, just off the coast of Spain, couple Paul and Barbara make their way to an otherworldly fishing village in search of assistance. By nightfall, things have taken a strange turn; the couple finds that the village is inhabited by humanoid fish creatures who serve Dagon, one of the old sea gods. Barbara is captured and used for an ancient ritual in which her naked body is lowered into the water to entice Dagon. Despite Paul's desperate attempts to save her, Barbara demands that he let her go to a watery grave. In his final stand against the cult, Paul sets himself on fire; the priestess overseeing the ritual leaps on him and pushes him into the water where he begins to transform into an amphibious creature. He smiles, accepting his fate as one of them.

Despite the fact that much of the plot follows *The Shadow Over Innsmouth*, there is a moment in the film's finale, during the encounter with Dagon, in which the film captures something of the earlier story from which the film takes its name:

> Then suddenly I saw it. With only a slight churning to mark its rise to the surface, the thing slid into view above the dark waters. Vast, Polyphemus-like, and loathsome, it darted like a stupendous monster of nightmares to the monolith, about which it flung its gigantic scaly arms, the while it bowed its hideous head and gave vent to certain measured sounds. I think I went mad then. (Lovecraft 2011 [1919]: 5)

The monstrous reveal of Dagon – a large tentacled creature in the film – marks an uncommon encounter with one of the elder gods, which are more often than not absent from films adapting Lovecraft's universe. Barbara's encounter with Dagon mostly takes place off-screen — coded visually as a rape by her ink-smeared body — yet her adamance that Paul let her die intimates towards the horror of her ordeal. After re-emerging from the water, Barbara hangs naked and limp from a winch and stares emptily away from Paul. She asks Paul to kill her, with a blank expression and lifeless tone serving as cues for the madness described by the narrator of the short story after their encounter with the deep one.

Finally, Gordon directed *Dreams in the Witch House* for *Masters of Horror*, this time with little assistance from his regular Lovecraft collaborators – though writer Denis Paoli returns, alongside Ezra Godden who played lead character Paul in *Dagon*. Gordon's episode finds graduate student Walter Gilman (Godden) beginning to question his sanity as he is plagued by a series of increasingly disturbing dreams concerning the seventeenth-century witch who used to live in his building. After a mother and her son move into the building, the dreams get increasingly worse for Walter, who realises too late that the witch has murderous plans against the trio. After receiving mixed reviews on release, *Masters of Horror* proved popular on DVD with several re-releases. By bringing together the work of some of horror's biggest names, the show offered a fan service to horror enthusiasts while validating the status of its participants, Gordon included, as "masters" of the genre.

If the initial success of post-*Re-Animator* Lovecraft films was mixed at best, many of them have gone on to enjoy more successful afterlives on home media. Linda Badley notes, in a chapter on horror and home video cultures, that "video, but DVD in particular, appeals to a domestic culture of collectors, students, critics and aspiring filmmakers who find the medium the ideal collectible and archive" (2010: 55). Mark Bernard corroborates Badley's view, expressing that "during the DVD era, [the] marginal behavior [of horror collectors] was brought into the mainstream by the release of more horror films on DVD" (2014: 57). For Badley and Bernard, the mainstreaming of horror collecting made possible by DVD distributors reflects horror's capital, both cultural and economic, within the home video market. It also, importantly, reflects the journey of Gordon's films from obscurity to cult appreciation. As Bernard writes:

> [The] remaking or remediation of a film on DVD as a work of art becomes particularly interesting when marginal fare, such as horror and other exploitation film, is released on DVD. If the sell-through mandate mainstreamed the type of collecting

behavior normally reserved for 'cultish' audiences, it also mainstreamed some marginal genres and turned these products into 'art-objects'". (58)

Bernard's comments might be readily transposed onto any one of Gordon's Lovecraft films, which have each found an audience on home media due to their being re-packaged and re-released for the collector's market.

It is certainly possible that Gordon's status as the director of *Re-Animator* and, to a slightly lesser extent, *From Beyond* has inspired or at least informed the belated success of his smaller films on home release, including both his other Lovecraft films (*Castle Freak* and *Dagon*) as well as other titles such as *Robot Jox*, *The Pit and the Pendulum* and *Space Truckers* which have all received similar releases targeting the collectors' market. Indeed, it might be the case that there has been something of a snowball effect in terms of Gordon's reception on home media, that in the aftermath of the rapid cultification of *Re-Animator* his other films were re-positioned as cult texts also. Whether or not this has been the case, one can plausibly observe in his Lovecraft films alone the sustained vision of a B-horror auteur approaching Lovecraft in a casually reverent but fundamentally unserious way, perhaps to consciously reflect the grand pomposity of the source material itself. Moreover, across a series of five Lovecraft films Gordon shows a recurring interest in maintaining his "ensemble company", to keep it in the family, so to speak, by working with familiar collaborators both on- and off-screen. The recurring involvement of cast members Jeffrey Combs and Barbara Crampton, as well as crew members Brian Yuzna, Charles, Albert, and Richard Band and Dennis Paoli, among others, creates mild cohesion, both aesthetic and industrial, between his Lovecraft adaptations. Despite merits in all offerings, it feels fair to write that Gordon's Lovecraft films do vary somewhat in quality, from the heights of *Re-Animator* to lesser adaptations such as *Castle Freak*. Nevertheless, Gordon's status as film's great Lovecraft adapter remains intact, represented by a deliriously inventive, gruesomely gory and markedly funny body of work that displays various Lovecraftian elements as well as several auteurist qualities from Gordon. While it is possible to trace the genealogy of Gordon's career following *Re-Animator* as symptomatic of the film's success — not to mention the careers of others key players, including Yuzna, Combs and Crampton — it is far from the film's only legacy; as I have suggested already, the cult capital of *Re-Animator* is multifaceted and enduring, as the next and final chapter will seek to explore in more detail.

FOOTNOTES

36. Lovecraft died as a result of cancer of the small intestine in 1937 at the age of 46.
37. For my purposes, I have chosen to focus on direct adaptations of Lovecraft and not on the deluge of films that have been clearly influenced by his works. These include films such as *Alien* and *The Thing*, as well as lesser known films such as *Leviathan* (George P. Cosmatos, 1989), *Dark Waters* (Mariano Baino, 1994), *Prometheus*, *Beyond the Gates* (Jackson Stewart, 2016), *The Void* (Steven Kotstanski and Jeremy Gillespie, 2016) and *The Endless* (Justin Benson and Aaron Moorhead, 2017), which all have distinct Lovecraftian elements. I have also chosen not to include films that are related to his works but not direct adaptations of particular stories, such as *Cast a Deadly Spell* (Martin Campbell, 1991), *In the Mouth of Madness* (John Carpenter, 1994) and *The Cabin in the Woods*.
38. See, Gordon (2018). Also, despite del Toro's ongoing obstacles with regards to *At the Mountains of Madness*, there are arguably relatively clear Lovecraftian elements in other films of his, including *Hellboy* (2004), *Crimson Peak* (2015), and *The Shape of Water* (2017).
39. As per the above table, this assessment excludes films without a direct textual point-of-reference, therefore a film such as *Alien*, which is less an adaptation of Lovecraft than a film significantly influenced by his work, does not fit the bill despite being a moderately-sized Fox production.
40. See US distributor Shout Factory's home releases of *The Curse*, for instance.
41. Moore has grappled with Lovecraft (with artist Jacen Burrows) in *The Courtyard* (2003) and *Neonomicon* (2010). Their most recent opus, *Providence* (2015-7), is well worth seeking out as an excellent example of Lovecraft in transcultural adaptation.
42. See *The Endless* for an example of a horror film that I would argue comes close to reaching what is referred to by Joshi as Lovecraftian cosmicism.
43. Hill is notably absent from Lovecraft's story in all but the name of a very minor character.
44. For similar work, see my own chapter on Spike Jonze's *Where the Wild Things Are* as a work that spans generations and employs critical reflexivity in its features (2019: 33-45).
45. It is worth also noting that Gordon planned to adapt "The Lurking Fear", another Lovecraft short story, before those plans were scuppered by the collapse of EIP (qtd in Jay, Dewey, Shumate 2013: 213). The film was later made under Band's next studio, Full Moon, where it was directed by C. Courtney Joyner.
46. Hickinbottom argues that, for Miike, a notably varied director, "the horror paradigm has functioned as a principal [economic] framework within which Miike has been understood in Western film discourse" (2020: 98).
47. It is worth noting that Arrow Video released a four film DVD boxset entitled *Fantastic Factory Presents…* (2011) which collects *Faust: Love of the Damned*, *Arachnid* (Jack Sholder 2001), *Beyond Re-Animator*, and *Romasanta: The Werewolf Hunt* (Paco Plaza, 2004).

Chapter Five: "He's Dead?" ... "Not Anymore!" The Cult Legacies of *Re-Animator*

Identifying 'Quality' Horror: Retrospection, Reappraisal and the Transcultural Legacy of *Re-Animator*

In reference to *Re-Animator*'s perverse sexual content and bloody appeal, producer Brian Yuzna has been quoted saying "it's what we call 'psycho-fiction', traumas can be a lot of fun" (qtd in Mathijs and Sexton 2011: 161). Yuzna — following a successful professional directorial debut with the equally gruesome and similarly cultist sex cult horror *Society* in 1989 — would go on to explore these themes further in sequels to *Re-Animator*, *Bride of Re-Animator* in 1990 and *Beyond Re-Animator* in 2003. Illustrated by the film's regular inclusion in guides to cult cinema,[48] *Re-Animator*'s particular brand of perverse "fun" has developed a currency with horror audiences that has traversed generations. The cultification of any film can be a hard thing to trace and may be the result of many factors, yet Yuzna's statement on psycho-fiction and the fun of trauma is, in fact, a useful starting point for ascertaining the possible reasons for *Re-Animator*'s endurance as a key cult horror film. And it has certainly endured.[49] For Mathijs and Xavier Mendik, what they refer to as "the anatomy of cult film" can be marked by a number of factors that include: innovation, badness, transgression, genre, intertextuality, "loose ends", nostalgia and gore (2008: 2-4). For the purposes of analysing *Re-Animator*'s textual and cult anatomy, I will use Mathijs's and Mendik's rubric to assess its credentials.

Cult Characteristic	Evidence in *Re-Animator*
Innovation	For Mathijs and Mendik, innovation comes by way of "instigating "new techniques" (2008: 2). *Re-Animator*'s central showcasing of gory effects, followed by its discursive positioning as a key 1980s gore film, marks out its innovation on Mathijs and Mendik's terms.
Badness	Unlike some cult films, *Re-Animator* has largely been on the receiving end of positive reviews, a factor that has been instrumental in establishing its status as a "quality" text among "lesser" works.

Transgression	This moves from a matter of "quality" to a matter of taste. The case for *Re-Animator*'s tastelessness is marked by its sexual perversity and ultraviolence, a theme deployed throughout, especially in regards to Hill's sexual and violent obsession with Megan.
Genre	Horror has forever been a key genre for cult appreciation, and the terms have often (though incorrectly) been conflated. Mathijs and Sexton identify that "a more specific use of the term cult horror refers to one period in the history of horror cinema that has become a cult in itself […] roughly from the mid 1970s to the late 1980s" (2011b: 195), the period in which *Re-Animator* firmly sits.
Intertextuality	As I have already explored in this book, *Re-Animator* readily employs intertextual elements that signpost horror cinema's dynamic past and lucrative then-present. Indeed, Mathijs and Sexton include the film in their discussion of 1980s cult horror, stating that "by the second half of the 1980s […] highly mannerist exercises in gore began to overshadow the subcultural and counter-cultural aspects of the cult of horror. Extremely violent and highly intertexual homages such as *Re-Animator*, *Return of the Living Dead* or *The Hitcher* continued to attract cultist receptions" (2011b: 198).
"Loose Ends"	For Mathijs and Mendik, "loose ends" refer to censored content that completists often seek out (2008: 3). *Re-Animator* exists in many versions. In the UK, for instance, the BBFC (British Board of Film Certification) demanded cuts of up to a couple of minutes to be taken from the film's more gory and sexually-violent content. The film has since been readily available uncut in many territories, but its timely alignment with the cut and/or banned video nasties of the 1980s has formed part of its cult reputation as a problem film. It is worth noting that *Re-Animator* was never banned by the BBFC and therefore is not an official video nasty.
Nostalgia	Nostalgia brings together all the factors above, and is perhaps best represented by *Re-Animator*'s enduring popularity on home release, a matter that will be discussed at greater length later in this chapter.
Gore	Lawrence O'Toole captures, in his 1979 article "The Cult of Horror", the basis of horror's transgressive appeal: "with society a circus of sensations, anything truly terrifying is saliva for a jaded palette" (2008: 260). Horror's tendency towards hardcore content, or gore, has often been found to be the basis on which its cult status has been erected. It also needs no qualification that *Re-Animator* is a gory film.

Table 5.1 — A survey of the cult characteristics of Re-Animator

Table 5.1 shows the various ways in which *Re-Animator* intersects with conceptualisations of the cult film, with the notable exception of badness due to the film's reception as a good film of its sort. And while Mathijs and Mendik make no indication that *all* of their criteria must be satisfied, it is interesting to consider *Re-Animator*'s "quality" as the platform on which its enduring popularity has been mounted, especially given the persistence of the bad/good equivalence that prevails in the practice of cultification. Perhaps more than any other genre, horror films have been subject to critical snobbery which has paved the way for re-evaluations seeking to retroactively reposition particular texts as films of value. Indeed, much of the work of cult film studies — a field within which *Re-Animator* can be easily positioned — has gone to lengths to explain the unrecognised qualities of neglected films. Of course, such determination comes with all the expected problems associated with canonisation: critical biases, narrow representation and good, old-fashioned collective snobbery. However, by general consensus *Re-Animator* was far from the bad film that sometimes leads a title to be adopted by cult film fans. Consider the following, a selection of excerpts from contemporary reviews of *Re-Animator*:

> "Close to being a silly ghoulie classic – the bloodier it gets, the funnier it is" (Pauline Kael, 1985).

> "In its own way, on its own terms, in its corrupt genre, this movie worked as well as any other movie [at Cannes]" (Roger Ebert, *Chicago Sun Times*, 1985).

> "*Re-Animator* has as much originality as it has gore, and that's really saying something. Stay away if you haven't a special fondness for severed body parts" (Janet Maslin, *New York Times*, 1985).

> "It's simply the best, funniest Grand Guignol horror picture to come along in ages (Kevin Thomas, *Los Angeles Times*, 1985).

The critical consensus at the time of release was that *Re-Animator* is a film of quality, an instant "classic" in fact, in the words of Pauline Kael. Roger Ebert's original review was submitted after its screening at Cannes, arguably the most prestigious of film festivals on the world circuit. Oh, the horror! If the chorus of approval that the film was met with is taken as a marker of its quality, then *Re-Animator* was already doing something that few horrors outside of prestige studio pictures such as *Rosemary's Baby* and *The Exorcist* were capable of doing, which is to appeal to audiences beyond the regular genre crowd. As a horror film on the festival circuit, *Re-Animator* began as a transgressive film in the context of regular festival sensibilities, which favour films with dramatic substance over the attractions of a splatter film, at least outside of horror festivals. Therefore, it is worth noting that *Re-Animator*'s first act of transgression, a frequent component of cult reputations, per Mathijs and Mendik, stems from the film's initial point of contact at Cannes.

Re-Animator's quality, however, though immediately recognised on horror terms, runs counter to what is usually recognised as a great film. It both corresponds with and challenges Jeffrey Sconce's notion of the "counter-cinema", represented by an alternative academy of trash connoisseurs whose canon is cultivated "from the dregs of exploitation" (2010: 113), which champion "reading strategies that render the bad into the sublime" (119). *Re-Animator* is, indeed, exploitation of a sort, but as the contemporary reviews of the film make clear, it is hardly illustrative of what one might construe as the "dregs" of its genre. Rather, it is the opposite; an exemplar work of an at times lurid, and certainly luridly-imagined, genre that gets bashed by conservative critics with the power to influence taste. Of course, there have been various cult films that are both popularly and historically regarded as quality works. And while the notion of quality does not always sit well within all cult circles, quality cult films do exist; Mathijs and Sexton, for example, have identified that "films such as *The Wizard of Oz* or *Casablanca* have been enjoyed as cult by generations of audiences" (2011: 17).[50] The transcultural adoption of particular films into particular spectatorial paradigms, then, is not always dependent on badness or critical neglect, but can be due to other factors such as those detailed in the table above. As such, *Re-Animator*'s cultification has occurred in spite of its quality within the context of the genre (or subgenre) in which it features, and it is not in need of critical legitimacy in the way that some other horror films are.

There is a moment of recognition of *Re-Animator*'s cult status in Sam Mendes's Oscar-winner *American Beauty* (1999) in which drifting middle-ager Lester shares a joint with Ricky, the teenager next door who happens to be infatuated with Lester's daughter. Alan Ball's script reads thus:

LESTER

What about... did you ever see that one movie, with the body walking around holding its own head? And then the head went down on that babe?

RICKY

Re-Animator. It was okay.

(*American Beauty* Screenplay, 1999: 36)

Later, *Re-Animator* is used as short-hand by Lester for a desired drug exchange with Ricky. However, Lester's initial reference to *Re-Animator* is intriguing, and for more than merely seeming incongruous in what is otherwise a serious drama taking aim at the vacant shell of the American Dream. In the chronology of his self-destruction, Lester's reference to *Re-Animator* comes just as he begins to wobble on the cliff edge of his mundane, suburban existence, and therefore corresponds with his increasing desire to let loose and relapse into his younger self by taking it easy, talking film, smoking pot and lusting after women – the latter impulse is expressed in his boyish memory of "the head [that] went down on that babe". More than just cement its status as a cult film, which *American Beauty*'s citation of *Re-Animator* arguably does, this scene expresses a feeling towards 1980s horror, that it is problematic in its content, but that it is also a site of refuge for those who remember it fondly.

Re-Animator is a curious text among cult horror films. It has neither the heritage status of, say, *The Cabinet of Dr. Caligari* (Robert Weine, 1920) or *Freaks* (Tod Browning, 1932), nor the transgeneric acclaim of canon horror films such as *Night of the Living Dead* or *The Exorcist*. It has neither the outright independence of *Halloween*, the transnational appeal of *Suspiria* (Dario Argento, 1977), nor the midnight-movie exhibition context of *Eraserhead* (David Lynch, 1977). It has neither the outright controversy of *Cannibal Holocaust* (Ruggero Deodato, 1980), nor the so-bad-it's-good charm of *Troll 2* (Drake Floyd, 1990). It was neither a video nasty nor a grindhouse horror film; it was transgressive but not totally outrageous; it was intentionally, and not accidentally, funny, and was unusually accomplished for a 1980s horror film. Despite the fact that *Re-Animator* might seem to be a hard film to situate within regular cult paradigms, its cultist characteristics and enduring success across media has cemented a legacy as one of the key films of a period that was marked out as focal to the cult of horror:

> Throughout much of the 1980s, this arrangement of subculture, counter culture and popular culture around horror extended into a veritable cult industry. New production, distribution, and promotion practices, combined with innovative modes of reception, helped establish a worldwide fascination with the horror genre that spawned celebrations of the most diverse kinds. (Mathijs and Sexton 2011: 197)

What, then, should we make of *Re-Animator* today? It remains, to this day, gloriously gory, consciously camp, frequently funny and interminably quotable; it has intelligence, nostalgia and intertextual currency that is consistent with particular forms of cult fandom. This chapter will go on to examine the cultural legacies embodied in the sequels, adaptations and parodies that the film has inspired, but what is clear already is that there is still much for audiences to take from *Re-Animator*, elements that reflect its transcultural standing and enduring status as a cult film.

Re-Animator's Legacy on Home Media

I.Q. Hunter, in a chapter concerning cult fandoms and the intertextual possibilities provided by paratextual engagements with Stanley Kubrick's *2001: A Space Odyssey* (1968), summarises the relationship between fan and text in the following way:

> Encountering [a] film – which is to say, re-encountering it – can be life-changing and transfiguring if the viewer is able to submit, to think and to *care* […] [the] notion of emotional investment in a film, obvious as it is with cult films, emphasizes how much of our relationship with films is defined by what might seem intrinsic to adaptation – intertextual adventures across paratexts, pursuing allusions, comparisons, precursors, add-ons of all kinds. It is a relationship of *care* that takes place over *time*, from anticipation of the film to embedded knowledge of it. Cultists care for texts in relationships of memory, nostalgia and anticipation; they have emotional investments in films, a sense even of ownership; they pursue the extratextual and seemingly irrelevant, specialize in breaking the boundaries of texts, and enthusiastically explore intertextual worlds, including texts that might further explicate bewildering films. (2016: 137, all emphases original)

Hunter's description illustrates a range of interesting characteristics of the cult enthusiast. What can be construed from his observations is that there emerges a very particular, indeed privileged, type of relationship between cultists and the texts they cherish. In this extract, Hunter pays close attention to the interstitial aspects of fandom, in what happens beyond the confines of an adored text once a committed enthusiast has found a desire (or even a need) to "break the boundaries" of it.

This process is what Hunter terms "intertextual adventures across paratexts", and he describes "add-ons of all kinds" as fundamental aspects to cult engagement with a text. These paratexts, from DVD releases to various other types of tie-in, are fascinating artefacts that demonstrate the numerous ways in which fandoms adopt a text and disseminate it through the relevant (sub)cultures. Indeed, Tamao Nakahara writes that "as films become more integrated into popular memory and new forums such as fan sites and DVD commentaries increasingly have become part of the filmic experience, film historical and analytical practices must follow suit in their study of the intertextually connected media" (2010: 150). While Nakahara's comments capture radically transforming viewing cultures, they also observe an increasingly cineliterate audience made possible by the ready availability of extratextual "add-ons", to use Hunter's term.

In the context of a viewing market increasingly saturated with readily available special features, there is nothing particularly special about one's fandom for the simple fact of watching a few extras. Other tactics for developing a cultist mode of reception include a rapidly expanding market for collector's editions with increasing amounts of content and marked by increasing cost and/or scarcity. Kate Egan, using the example of Vipco's VHS and DVD re-releases of the video nasties, writes that "what the reciprocal discursive connections between Vipco and the nasty titles seem to illustrate is the commercial benefits, for both company and product, of carving out a niche commercial image based around notions of the anachronistic, the retro or 'stylised nostalgia'" (2007: 192). What emerges from a survey of the different types of home release – marked, variously, by region, content, cost and scarcity – is different degrees of engagement.

Even concerning *Re-Animator*'s release since the advent of DVD, there are now three cuts widely available to choose from – the unrated theatrical cut, an R-rated cut intended for the video market and a longer "Integral Cut" which boasts additional footage previously unseen before its restoration and release for the home market. In a chapter on the twenty-fifth anniversary release of The Exorcist, which was marked by the release of the tantalisingly-titled "Version You've never Seen", Michael Arnzen captures the subcultural capital of such releases:

> The phrase "The Version You've Never Seen!" is clearly a creative marketing ploy, directly addressing the potential spectator in second person ("you"), imperative ("!"), in an attempt to pique curiosity taken straight out of the ballyhoo tactics of early horror filmmakers like William Castle. By flaunting something that's implicitly been withheld from view, it appeals to the voyeuristic desire of the horror audience, suggesting that this version of the film harbors an unseen secret. And like a sideshow carnival barker, it almost dares audiences to peek inside the tent and discover a new experience. (2004: 102)

The compulsive act of collecting of *all* things in relation to a particular film is about more than curiosity; for those enthusiastically invested in a text, it is about being a completist, an expert, by mastering the text through knowing all its elements and collecting it in abundance.

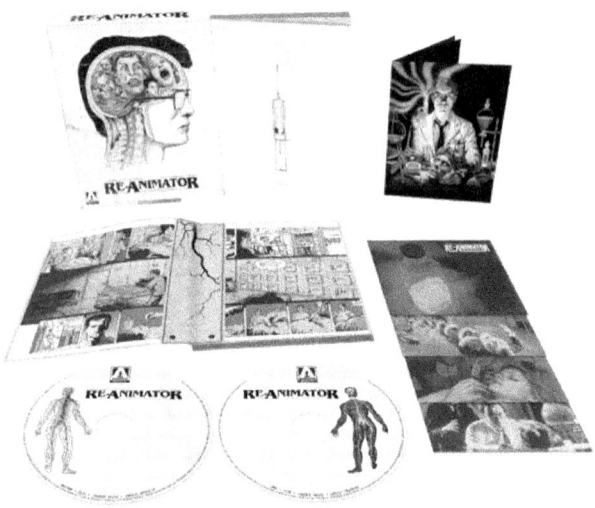

Fig. 5.1 – The contents of Arrow Video's 2017 lavish limited release of Re-Animator © *Arrow Films.*

It is worth noting that a key context for watching – or, indeed, re-watching – *Re-Animator* today has been enabled by its substantial success on home release formats, releases that have made various attempts to tie up the "loose ends", to use Mathijs and Mendik's term, left by pre-exisiting cuts deemed incomplete. Beside other popular releases, including a delightful steel book limited edition released by Second Sight for the UK market, *Re-Animator* was subject to the limited-edition treatment by Arrow Video in 2017. The release was limited to 10,000 units and included two versions of the film (an 86-minute unrated version and a 105-minute "integral" version), both remastered in 4K. The release was bound in deluxe packaging that included newly commissioned artwork by Justin Erickson, as well as a collectable booklet that included new writing by Michael Gingold and a copy of Steven Jones and Christopher Jones's 1991 comic adaptation. The release boasted a wealth of extra features, including new interviews and documentaries, as well as deleted scenes and TV spots.

Prestige releases of films such as *Re-Animator* are important to its establishment and enduring status as a classic horror film. As Linda Badley observes in her chapter on the role that home releasing has played in horror's development, prestige releases (such as those by Criterion)[51] and serious contemplation (such as that offered by *Video Watchdog*) "treated the home viewer as a discriminating collector, scholar, and critic", complementing one another by "applying auteurist standards to international cult and exploitation films maimed by territorial censors and ignored by critics" (2010: 48-9). It is evident that the style of a film's preservation and re-release precedes and/or complements its reputation as a cult film and, if necessary, its critical reappraisal. Prestige releases do much to overturn canonical biases and return favour to neglected and/or marginalised films. Building on Egan's aforementioned work, Mark McKenna argues as much, stating that:

> though processes of cultural distinction have historically separated these cinemas based upon preconceived valorisations, in recent years an increased convergence of these markets has been observed. This is largely commercially driven, with distributors reinforcing, extending and challenging traditional notions of what might constitute the canonical film, and consequently further augmenting how ideas of value are constructed for films which fall outside mainstream consumption. (2017: 32)

More than that, however, such releases constitute a substantial source of real capital for a film. Take Arrow Video's limited-edition release of *Re-Animator*, for example, which is sold out and changes hands on eBay for prices in the region of $125.[52] Measured against the film's theatrical box office (as explored in chapter three), and taking into account that this is just one example of *Re-Animator*'s presence on home release formats, this marks a new way of quantifying a film's financial return. Arrow Video have since released a regular edition of *Re-Animator* on Blu-ray and DVD, while Second Sight have overseen the film's UK releases, which included the aforementioned limited steel book edition. Meanwhile, Capelight oversaw the release of a German limited edition of the film, as well as a *trilogie* boxset that comes in VHS packaging, therefore tapping into another key source of cultural capital, the nostalgia for antiquated release formats.[53] One can see how this data might transform understandings of a film's financial success.

It is worth also taking a moment to consider that Arrow Video's limited-edition treatment is saved only for its "biggest" titles, which must be treated as a structuring element for the film's reception on these home formats. Other titles that have been subject to this form of prestige release include canon horror films such as *Carrie*, *An American Werewolf in London* and *The Thing*, as well as classic works of world horror and exploitation, such as the films of Dario Argento (*The Bird With the Crystal Plumage* [1969]; *Cat O' Nine Tails* [1971]; *Deep Red* [1975]; and *Phenomena* [1985]), Wes Craven (*The Last House on the Left* [1972]; *The Hills Have Eyes* [1977]), Lucio Fulci (*City of the Living Dead* [1980]), David Cronenberg (*Videodrome* [1983]), and Jörg Buttgereit (*Nekromantik* [1987]). Even *Re-Animator*'s own sequel, Brian Yuzna's *Bride of Re-Animator*, has been subject to Arrow Video's special treatment.[54] So, building upon McKenna's assessment of how such releases work to overturn critical biases against marginalised genre films, one might observe that even in the context of Arrow Video's own releases, the process by which distribution companies select films for limited edition treatment conveys taste hierarchies and tactics of cultification that illustrate the development of a sub-canon in its own right, one that elevates certain films over others. The home release dynamics of *Re-Animator*, which has accorded the film heightened visibility among horror fans, is without doubt a key context for its continued success and attendant positioning within the landscape of 1980s horror and current cultures of horror viewing and appreciation.

"Adventures Across Paratexts": Sequels, Spin-Offs, Porn Parodies – and a Musical

Re-Animator's endurance has been marked by a consistent fanbase exhibiting cultist forms of reception and appreciation, which demonstrates its sustained cultural significance while re-mediating it to the centre of an intertextual, and intermedial, constellation of texts. For many, *Re-Animator*'s textual legacy ended with the release of its second sequel, *Beyond Re-Animator* in 2003; however, *Re-Animator*'s legacy extends further by some degrees. This section will therefore trace the variety of directions in which the source film has been opened out to incorporate various forms of textual expansion that includes sequels, spin-offs, parodies and more.

As discussed in chapter four in regard to *Re-Animator* as a work of adaptation, *Bride of Re-Animator* makes use of some of the narrative elements that were unused in the original film. *Bride of Re-Animator*, therefore, has a role to play in one's approach to the boundaries of the text (to follow Hunter once again) as a work of adaption, and becomes a key component in the expanding intertextual world of *Re-Animator*. For Carolyn Jess-Cooke, sequels have a functional role to play in the development of a participatory culture surrounding a film:

> The sequel operates in conjunction with genre to facilitate discourse, institutional practices and spectatorial engagement – to heighten, in short, each other's aesthetic and industrial imperatives [...] by engaging audiences within the stabilizing framework of a sequel, the sequel effectively markets, interprets, substantiates and re-identifies generic cues, texts and origins, thereby promising a much more participatory experience. (2009: 53)

Jess-Cooke's conception of sequels takes into account both economic imperatives and modes of consumption; indeed, in her analysis of sequels to slasher horror films (of particular use here), she writes that such films "exploit and contribute to the sequel's (perceived) function as a mode of cannibalising old stories, zombie-fying dead texts, and altogether 'slashing' traditional forms of originality" (53). Even the title of the film serves as evidence of Yuzna's (severed-)tongue-in-cheek approach to the series, as it demonstrates an intertextual function as both a sequel to *Re-Animator* and an update of *Frankenstein* and *Bride of Frankenstein*, the sequel that *Bride of Re-Animator* quite evidently homages/parodies.

Bride of Re-Animator opens *in media res* months after the climactic massacre at the Miskatonic Institute. The action commences in the midst of the Peruvian Civil War where West and Cain are continuing their research on the dismembered parts of soldiers. Upon their return to the Miskatonic Institute, the pair soon find themselves subject to suspicion as a local policeman, Lieutenant Chapman, becomes increasingly interested in body parts that went missing in the aftermath of the massacre. West kills the investigator during an altercation, before attempting to revive him with his new and improved re-agent. In the meantime, another scientist, Dr. Graves, has found and successfully (re-)re-animated the head of Hill who, aided by the power of mesmerism, commands Chapman to force Graves to attach wings to his neck (bringing to mind the iconic bolts of Frankenstein's monster). In his laboratory, West has made attempts at creating the titular "bride" using the heart of Megan combined with the body parts of other women that he has acquired along the way. Cain is naturally repulsed by West's creation and his new girlfriend, Francesca, fights it. The "bride", powered by the engine of Megan's heart, is crushed by Cain's rejection and destroys herself. As this is all happening, Hill uses his powers to summon a horde of re-animated bodies to attack West and the others, forcing them to escape through the crypt of the cemetery that backs onto his laboratory. As the crypt collapses, Cain and Francesca manage to escape while West is trapped underground with Hill and his horde.

Of course, West survives. The second sequel, *Beyond Re-Animator*, picks up thirteen years later and finds West in prison for his not insubstantial crimes. From the confines of his cell, West has not only found himself able to experiment on rats, but also to make further progress with his re-agent, which attracts the interest of the new prison doctor, Dr. Howard Philips, so named for H. P. Lovecraft himself. After the death of his girlfriend at the hands of an infatuated prison guard (a theme that recalls Hill's violent obsession with Megan in the first film), Philips performs a re-animation on her with West. The two are caught by the prison warden who is then killed by West before he subsequently, you guessed it, re-animates him. For the warden's re-animation, West experiments by using the re-agent he developed with the rats; unsurprisingly, this re-animation causes a more volatile reaction which leads to an outbreak within the prison. During the riot caused by the outbreak, West escapes while pretending to be Philips. The authorities arrive just as

West disappears into the night, bound for horizons not yet known.

Despite attempts to elevate both films to cult status by subsequent home releases – most notably Arrow Video's deluxe treatment of *Bride of Re-Animator* and Vestron's equivalent for *Beyond Re-Animator* – neither is remembered half as fondly as Gordon's original film. Echoing Jess-Cooke's previous comments, Stuart Henderson, in his discussion of the *Scream* franchise (1996-2011), notes that "in the sequel form there is a tendency for what was novel to become formulaic, for variation to become repetition" (2014: 155). That is not to say that *Re-Animator*'s two sequels are without merit; both are fun expansions of the universe, making excellent use of Combs, and – in the case of *Bride of Re-Animator* particularly – showing creativity in their utilisation of the remains of Lovecraft's story.[55] Overall, by the very fact of the reasonable stretches of time between their productions, *Re-Animator*'s sequels demonstrate the original film's enduring impact on the horror genre. Moreover, they provide evidence of the ways in which sequels both compound economic modalities while attending to fans' desires to engage with the source – simply put, they create a filmic universe out of a single text that, in correspondence with the Lovecraft story, re-mediates it to the epicentre of a developing intertextual enterprise.

A slightly different form of paratextual expansion comes in the form of a series of comics produced by Adventure Comics in the aftermath of *Bride of Re-Animator*'s release. In the first sequence, a three-issue run created by writer Steven Jones and artist Christopher Jones, the *Re-Animator* comic largely stays true to the plot of Gordon's film. Moreover, Jones has clearly modelled the characters' looks on their filmic counterparts. Other limited runs include a one-shot titled *Re-Animator: Tales of Herbert West* (1991), which is more closely based on Lovecraft's short story, as well as *Re-Animator: Dawn of Re-Animator* (1992), a four-issue limited series written by Bill Spangler and illustrated by Jose Malaga, which serves as a prequel to Jones and Jones's earlier comic and, therefore, to the film also.

I would argue that these comics are functionally multi-purposed; they operate both independently of the film(s) and as a form of paratextual expansion; they are works of adaption; and they are also collectible, ephemeral objects for fans that play with and in the boundaries of the source text. In tandem with *Bride of Re-Animator*, the comics considered here (and that is without mentioning later runs of *Re-Animator* comics from other presses) reflect the *Re-Animator* cult while contributing to the budding franchise growing out of Gordon's original film. I.Q. Hunter describes *2001: A Space Odyssey* as "a marvellously bold and seemingly hermetic work of art", yet one that is also "not a stand-alone object" but "the dominant text in a process of textual production that engages audiences – or, at any rate, audiences willing to be engaged – in an intertextual odyssey" (2016: 138). While I would not be so bold as to suggest that *Re-Animator* entertains half the enigma, or indeed fandom, of *2001*, it seems fair to reflect on the fact that both films have been reworked through paratextual re-mediation in the form of sequels, novelisations, and other adjacent items of ephemera. Naturally, both films are fully able to, and do, operate independently of the wider textual universe, yet for those willing to follow the films' various textual threads there is an ever-expanding number of ways to do so.

It is the case that *Re-Animator* has been subject to some rather bizarre forms of paratextual adoption and adaptation. One of the more striking examples of these texts comes in the form of a porn parody, (in)appropriately titled *Re-Penetrator* (The Evil Carrot, 2004) from production company Burning Angel and starring cult porn star and entrepreneur Joanna Angel.[56] The film, which won an AVN industry award for Most Outrageous Sex Scene, finds Herbert Breast using his re-agent to resurrect a female cadaver. Naturally — this is pornography, after all — the corpse is injected with a heavy dose of sexual vigour and the couple spends most of the remaining running time engaging in all manners of sex (17 of 20 minutes). Star Joanna Angel told me that while *Re-Penetrator* was a huge success, it was also the source of much controversy upon release for breaching rules about uses of blood in pornographic films. In a Skype interview in October 2020, Angel revealed to me that *Re-Penetrator* "was actually too much for porn". Controversy is fitting for a porn parody of *Re-Animator*, as is *Re-Penetrator*'s enduring reputation as a cult film among porn fans.

The film is interesting for a number of reasons. Hunter, in a discussion on the audience of porn parody *Lord of the G-Strings: The Femaleship of the String* (Terry West, 2003), writes that "films like this embrace their viewers as savvy and discriminating insiders, honoured participants in an exclusive postmodern cult" (2016: 110). Likewise, in the case of *Re-Penetrator*, not only does the film's very existence confirm the (sub)cultural status of its source – as a cult text, no less, otherwise for whom is it being made? – its deviation from the plot of the film takes the text in new and interesting directions. In *Re-Penetrator*, Herbert Breast is attacked by the corpse at the point of ejaculation. He is gutted by the re-animated zombie-woman, who leaves his organs gorily scattered across the room. As Herbert Breast sits unable to re-animate his erection, the zombie-woman picks up his re-agent and turns smiling towards the camera. As Steve Jones writes, there is a striking inversion of the text in *Re-Penetrator*'s finale:

> It is Herbert's turn to become a sex-zombie. Herbert's death and her agency close the text, and the pop-shot's sovereignty is usurped by its gore-climax. *Re-Penetrator*'s horror consequently debunks the notion that porn is structured around male sexual pleasure. By combining sex and violence, *Re-Penetrator* upsets porn's normative conventions. (2013: 161)

It is worth noting that Jones is acutely sensitive to the problems that arise out of the coalescence of sex and violence in horror porn; nevertheless his reading of *Re-Penetrator*'s ending reveals how the adaptation engages with the source material in its scrutiny of the fragility of the male ego and sexual impotence, themes I considered in my analysis of *Re-Animator* in chapter two. Suffice it to say that given pornography's formal characteristics and primary affective goals, there must be a strong reason to sacrifice the money shot that concludes so many productions. That the makers of *Re-Penetrator* choose to do so, especially in a way that undermines Breast/West, must be reflective of a desire to re-work the material; therefore, in its conscious sacrifice of a climactic image of male sexual pleasure, *Re-Penetrator* (inadvertently or otherwise) offers a commentary on the power dynamics at work in the original film.

A less underground adaptation of *Re-Animator* arrived in 2011 in the form of a musical. *Re-Animator: The Musical* opened to critical acclaim at the Steve Allen Theatre in Los Angeles with a book that was written by original writers Stuart Gordon, Dennis Paoli and William J. Norris, accompanied by music and lyrics by Mark Nutter. *Re-Animator: The Musical* followed in the tradition of a small handful of other horror musical adaptions by creating a tongue-in-cheek homage to (and, in some ways, a parody of) the original film.[57] After premiering in Los Angeles, the show moved to New York and then Edinburgh where it opened to warm receptions. In a glowing *Variety* review, critic Bob

Verini writes of the show:

> Amid all the groany jokes, threadbare trappings, magic tricks and movie homages, Mark Nutter's score may be overlooked, and it shouldn't be. Synthesized with valiant gusto by musical whiz Peter Adams, it alternates mock-heroic anthems worthy of Bernard Herrmann's trunk with cute ditties in a Gilbert & Sullivan jugular vein, all teeming with tricky rhymes and wit. (2011)

As with the finale of *Re-Penetrator*, it is hard not to approach *Re-Animator: The Musical* as anything other than a conscious engagement with, and expansion of, the original text. While it understandably does not offer the erotic mode of participation provided by the porn parody, the musical engages the text in different ways, doubling down on its campiness to amplify its textual roots in classical horror cinema.

The re-mediation of a familiar story to an unlikely medium is always going to make an impact on its reception; indeed, as Barbara Wallace Grossman notes in regard to Julie Taymor's musical of *The Lion King*, "the story may be familiar, but how Taymor and her colleagues tell it is strikingly original, using a variety of theatrical techniques" (2017: 127). Accompanied by the interactive thrill of live gore effects, which ceremoniously splatter the front few rows of spectators during performances, the transposition of *Re-Animator* into musical theatre — which also brings to mind *The Rocky Horror Picture Show* (Jim Sharman, 1975), another point of influence for *Re-Animator* — represents yet another dramatic reworking of the text that brings it back to life in a newly mediated context. Indeed, the show's liveness adds certain new interactive and uniquely affective elements that go beyond the inclusion of musical numbers. As Julian Woolford writes of *The Producers*, "at the stage musical, audiences relished the intertextual pleasure of recognising the palimpsests of the original movie alongside the creative decisions and new experiences of text, song, staging and performance that the re-mediated musical afforded" (2017: 87). *Re-Animator: The Musical* reworks the film using the language and embodied affects of musical theatre; in doing so, the musical provides a new, re-mediated experience of a familiar text that is both cultist and adaptive in form, offering extratextual possibilities for enthusiastic fans willing to explore and participate in the text's legacy.

Re-Penetrator and *Re-Animator: The Musical* might not, at first, appear to share much in common — after all, one is an unauthorised underground adaptation while the other is a lavish stage event with the involvement of many of the film's original creators. Yet both texts demonstrate the reworking of a cult text by way of two formally disparate languages that each embellish the original film while offering new ways of reading it. In the various "adventures across paratexts", to once again use Hunter's phrase, that have been undertaken in this subsection, it is clear that *Re-Animator* is not a static text, but one that instead evolves as it opens out through intertextually aligned subsequent works.

CODA: THE CULT STARDOMS OF JEFFERY COMBS AND BARBARA CRAMPTON

While Stuart Gordon arguably remains the most vital player for spearheading what might be referred to as the Lovecraft revival of the mid-to-late-1980s, there is much to be said about the stardoms of Combs and Crampton that formed in the crucible of *Re-Animator*'s success. Combs obviously returned to the role of Herbert West twice, in *Bride of Re-Animator* and *Beyond Re-Animator*. He also starred in other Stuart Gordon films, including the aforementioned films *From Beyond*, *Robot Jox*, *The Pit and the Pendulum* and *Castle Freak*, as well as *Fortress*, *Edmund*, *Stuck* and *The Black Cat* (Gordon's second contribution to *Masters of Horror*). Some of these roles are more substantial than others — *From Beyond*, *Castle Freak* and *The Black Cat* are lead roles, while others are no more than cameos. Indeed, functionally speaking, even guest appearances (or cameos) go some way towards establishing a performer's stardom due to the intertextual traces they generate. Given that Combs's recognisability connects his role as West to the later films, all films with markedly cultist leanings, it is fair to make the assessment that Combs's stardom is accordingly cultist.

Combs's star image has evolved to encompass a range of extratextual elements drawn from his popularity as West. It is an evolution that corresponds with his recurrence in other Lovecraft films such as *Necronomicon* and *The Lurking Fear*, as well as roles in other cult films including *The Guyver* (Steven Wang and Screaming Mad George, 1991) and *Trancers 2* (Charles Band, 1991), and television roles including *Star Trek: Deep Space Nine* (CBS, 1993-9). Combs also appeared in other films that exhibit a reflexive approach to horror that was symptomatic of the success of Wes Craven's *Scream*. These films include *The Frighteners* (Peter Jackson, 1996), *I Still Know What You Did Last Summer* (Danny Cannon, 1998) and *House on Haunted Hill* (William Malone, 1999), all films that appear to be cashing in on Combs's capital as a cult horror actor following *Re-Animator*.

It is arguable that in some of Combs's subsequent performances, especially those horror roles that mostly clearly intersect with various facets of his star image as West, his star image (as West) remains visible beyond the diegetic confines of the performance. Both from earlier roles, such as his performance as Tillinghast in *From Beyond*, to later roles in films such as *The Frighteners* and *House on Haunted Hill*, West manifests in aspects of Combs's notably excessive performances. As such, West in part returns to the screen through films that intertextually align with *Re-Animator*, albeit in an altered and allusive fashion. It is clear that by the end of the 1990s, and certainly following the cementing of *Re-Animator*'s classic status within horror subcultures, Combs's star image had evolved to the point that it intersects with both the roles he was offered and the performances he delivered in those roles. It is interesting and, I contend, possible to read Combs's performances in this way, as a continuation of his markedly cultist star image that began with his stylised performance as West in *Re-Animator*. Sarah Thomas discusses the "spectacular" attraction of cult cameos, writing that:

> Through such sequences, the 'site' of the character can become excessive, extraordinary and spectacular. At times, the flow of the narrative effectively stops as actors are given space to celebrate the eccentricities of their individual and resonant star performance. (2013: 42)

Indeed, by reading Combs's performances in such a way that acknowledges them as celebrations of his stardom, one can see how performances might form intertextual traces that connect similarly ostentatious, generically-aligned roles in subsequent horror films.

Despite small roles in Brian De Palma's *Body Double* (1984) and *Fraternity Vacation* (James Frawley, 1985), a trashy sex comedy, Barbara Crampton's success similarly owed much to her breakout performances in *Re-Animator* and *From Beyond*. Despite featuring in various other horror films during the late-1980s, including a notable early performance in the fun and inventive horror-comedy *Chopping Mall* (Jim Wynorski,

1986), as well as small roles in films such as *Pulse Pounders* (Charles Band, 1988) and *Puppet Master* (David Schmoeller, 1989), it was really due to Gordon's films that Crampton became a familiar name in horror circles.

Indeed, Crampton returned to Gordon's Lovecraft universe with lead roles in *From Beyond* and *Castle Freak*, in which she acted opposite Combs. She also worked with Gordon again on mid-1990s sci-fi comedy *Space Truckers*. Unlike Combs, who was enjoying reasonable success in the 1990s, Crampton's status as a horror icon has been mostly marked by a late-career revival, evident in roles in *You're Next* (Adam Wingard, 2011), *The Lords of Salem* (Rob Zombie, 2012), *We Are Still Here* (Ted Geoghegan, 2015), *Tales of Halloween* (various, 2015), *Beyond the Gates* (Jackson Stewart, 2016) and *Puppet Master: The Littlest Reich* (Sonny Laguna and Tommy Wiklund, 2018), as well as a recurring role in season four of horror series *Channel Zero* (Syfy, 2016-8).

Crampton's re-emergence as an elder statesperson of recent horror no doubt corresponds directly with her status as a fondly-remembered cult icon of the 1980s. Indeed, as a marker of her increasing popularity during that period, in the year following *Re-Animator*'s release, Crampton starred in a *Playboy* photo shoot entitled "Simply Beastly" (1986), which capitalised on both her horror stardom as well as the substantial sex appeal that she no doubt had among horror fans. In a chapter on the cult horror stardom of Ingrid Pitt, Kate Egan observes that for many young male horror fans female stars can have substantial roles to play in their sexual development, writing that "Pitt is presented [...] as a figure that connects with memories of fans' sexual awakening during the 1970s" (2013: 216). The same might be true of Crampton for the 1980s; her appearance in *Playboy* at the very least supports the notion that her star image formed around her iconicity within the horror genre, as well as from her sex appeal. There is almost something invitingly Freudian about the way in which Crampton's transition from twentysomething sex icon to a more markedly maternal role in some of these more recent films (such as *You're Next* and *We Are Still Here*) can be mapped onto androcentric, sophomoric presumptions about horror fandom. To draw another interesting comparison to the stardom of Ingrid Pitt, Crampton has followed her example by transitioning into adjacent discursive sectors, namely horror criticism. Just as Pitt wrote for magazines and her own website (Egan 2013: 212-3), Crampton is now a regular writer for *Fangoria* since it relaunched in 2018 and has recently featured in *In*

Search of Darkness (David A. Weiner, 2019), a documentary surveying 1980s horror, and will star in an upcoming remake of *Castle Freak* that has been produced by *Fangoria*'s production arm.

Footnotes

48. See Ernest Mathijs's and Jamie Sexton's BFI companion, *100 Cult Films* (2011a). In popular criticism, see lists such as *Entertainment Weekly*'s feature "The Cult 25: The Essential Left-Field Movie Hits Since '83" (2008).
49. For more on this, see an original interview between myself and current *Fangoria* editor Phil Nobile Jr., included in this volume as an appendix.
50. There are other factors, beside quality, that influence a film's cult reception. Joanne Hollows, for instance, writes that while *Titanic* "might have a 'cult' following, [...] its associations with a feminine and 'mass' audience on one hand, and 'middle-brow' discourses of 'quality' on the other, mean that it is unlikely to be easily accepted into academic or popular cult canons" (2003: 38). Of course, for Hollows the principle concern here is the gendering of film cults, however she does shine a light on the tricky notion of quality, which often is at odds with cult legitimacy.
51. See also Klinger (2006: 61-4).
52. Arrow Video have since released a standard edition of *Re-Animator*, which includes a selection of the special features but not the limited edition packaging, booklets or postcards. The regular edition is still available here: https://www.arrowvideo.com/product/re-animator/843.
53. For more work on this phenomenon, see Jonathan Wroot's chapter, "Bloody Muscles on VHS: When Asia Extreme Met the Video Nasties" (2020: 107-23).
54. Arrow Video also released a special edition of Yuzna's directorial debut *Society*.
55. This is likely due to Lovecraft enthusiast Dennis Paoli's continued involvement as a writer on *Bride of Re-Animator*. Paoli is replaced for *Beyond Re-Animator* by first-time writer José Manuel Gómez.
56. Joanna Angel has developed something of a cult reputation for a series of porn parodies that began with *Re-Penetrator* and also include *The XXXorcist* (The Evil Carrot, 2006), *Evil Head* (The Evil Carrot, 2012) and *I Know Who You Fucked Last Halloween* (Joanna Angel, 2018).
57. For a preceding example of the horror musical, see *Evil Dead: The Musical* (2003) or *The Fly* (opera, 2008).

Conclusion: *Re-Animator* Today: The Continuing Cult of a Horror Classic

It is clear that *Re-Animator* continues to impact the genre, as well as appreciations of it, in a variety of ways. In 2007, Stuart Gordon and Brian Yuzna featured at the cult/horror-film-festival-cum-academic-conference Cine-Excess, where the duo engaged with *Re-Animator*'s legacy in a markedly academic context.[58] By virtue of the film's longevity in overlapping discursive spaces, demonstrated in various forms in chapter five but also in its reputation among critics, fans and now scholars, *Re-Animator* has finally been accepted into the horror canon as a "classic" text.[59] But what exactly determines classic status today in a genre as turbulent as horror? For a long time horror scholarship has privileged certain "serious" horror films at the cost of including other, outwardly lighter films. The abundance of scholarship levelled at, for example, *Rosemary's Baby*, *The Exorcist* and *The Shining*, over the gore-horror of the 1980s, is illustrative of a discursive bias towards films that more clearly resemble cognitive horror over body horror. To see just how persistent such scrutiny has been, look no further than the recent, and highly contentious, announcement of the arrival of "post-horror".[60] For many, this debate is little more than a petty reinstitution of critical bias against the horror genre, and yet it is clear that these scuffles over terminology are illustrative of a renewed focus on horror's various forms, histories and modes of reception. Perspectives on horror's history are continually being revised, drawing attention away from those canon texts aforementioned to explore wider discursive practices and modes of consumption. Works including, but not limited to, Mark Bernard's *Reselling the Splat Pack* (2011), Steve Jones's *Torture Porn: Popular Horror After Saw* and Johnny Walker's *Contemporary British Horror Cinema: Industry, Genre and Society* (2015) are providing new, revisionist perspectives on horror filmmaking that move past the centrality of particular texts to observe the wider machinations of the genre, the industries that produce it and the audiences that consume it.

It is amid these revisionist perspectives that a critical repositioning of *Re-Animator* belongs. In the aftermath of torture porn's meteoric and lucrative rise, it seems increasingly important to consider *Re-Animator*'s role in the turn towards gore. James

Kendrick, writing on the centrality of gore in 1980s horror, observes that "despite the wide range of horror subgenres and production cycles, all of them were bound together by a newly intensified emphasis on make-up special effects and explicit gore" (2016: 313). Similarly, Isabel Christina Pinedo writes of the rise of gore as a postmodern development, stating that from the 1980s onwards "gore—the explicit depiction of dismemberment, evisceration, putrefaction, and myriad other forms of boundary violations with copious amounts of blood—takes center stage" in American horror (2004: 92). It is clear to see the critical possibilities that might arise from tracing these formal developments and reconciling them with the preponderance of gore that hit the horror market in the early 2000s.

Re-Animator illustrates the formal development of the horror genre in many different ways, from the rise of gore effects to the emergence of reflexive (or meta-) horror-comedy. Concerning the former, new appreciations of the formal qualities of the "highly disreputable" but "culturally significant" slasher subgenre arose out of Wickham Clayton's edited collection *Style and Form in the Hollywood Slasher Film* (2015a: 14).[61] These perspectives, though differently directed, demonstrate how horror studies is slowly opening out to account for the importance of body horror as well as its more cerebral (and, therefore, critically lauded) cousins. Speaking to the former, there is a clear correspondence between *Re-Animator*'s farcical homage to earlier horror traditions and the meta-horror represented by the likes of *Scream* just over a decade later. Fran Pheasant-Kelly observes in *Scream* that the film's "recognition as being postmodern arises from its self-referentiality and attention to intertextual details" (2015: 153). It is evident in *Re-Animator* that, genealogically speaking, intertextuality or meta-horror precedes the 1990s turn towards postmodernism in horror and has its roots in earlier contexts of horror production. These works therefore demonstrate the potential and need for horror studies to avoid perpetuating the problems associated with critical elitism and canonisation and to regard horror in ways that account for its plurality and modes of reception.

So, what is to be made of *Re-Animator* today, more than 35 years after its initial release? It is clear that the film continues to pervade horror discourse in multifaceted and multifarious ways. For many, *Re-Animator* remains a foundational text for horror fans that brings together various historical contexts, from the classic campiness of Universal's monster movies of the 1930s, to the slashers of the 1970s, the gore-horror films of the 1980s and the reflexive meta-horror films of the 1980s onwards. Its enduring impact has been marked by two sequels spread across a period of 18 years, a legacy in Lovecraft adaptation for its director and producer, an assortment of paratexts that include comics, a porn parody and a musical, cult stardom for two of its leads and even a citation in an Oscar-winning drama, *American Beauty*. *Re-Animator*'s legacy, then, is clearly a complex thing that encompasses a range of formal, historical and theoretical contexts, as I have attempted to shed light on over the course of this book. Is *Re-Animator* dead? Not so long as we, true to West's form, collectively continue to give it life.

Footnotes

58. For mention of Gordon and Yuzna's appearance, see Mendik (2020: 65). Further, at Cine-Excess 2007 Stuart Gordon also screened his film *Edmund* (2006).
59. It features in the coffee-table book as one the *101 Horror Films You Must See Before You Die* (Schneider, 2009).
60. See Steve Rose (2016: n.p.).
61. In his analysis of *Friday the 13th Part V: A New Beginning* (released in 1985, incidentally the same year as *Re-Animator*), Clayton makes the case for the potential for experimentation in a genre that is otherwise subject to "base connotations as low art" (2015b: 37). See also, *SEE! HEAR! CUT! KILL!: Experiencing Friday the 13th* (Clayton 2020).

Appendix: Insights into the Landscape of 1980s Horror: An Interview with *Fangoria* editor-in-chief Phil Nobile Jr (2018–)

For many horror fans, *Fangoria* was the jewel in the crown of magazine-based horror fandom. In its first run, over the course of 344 issues released between 1979 and 2015, *Fangoria* provided the final word on horror media. After closing its doors in 2015, *Fangoria* returned a few years later in 2018 under the editorship of Phil Nobile Jr, interviewed here. This interview was conducted via email correspondence in 2019.

Eddie Falvey: The rise of *Fangoria* coincided with substantial changes that were happening across the landscape of American horror, namely the development of different platforms of horror consumption such as VCR technology. What role do you think *Fangoria* had to play in horror's transformation during that period, do you think its role has changed since its revival and how important do you think it has been to the success and/or development of the horror genre?

Phil Nobile Jr: It's possibly a chicken/egg scenario, but my own experience was that initially in the '80s you found the movies out in the wild. They were at the drive-in or on the video shelf, but you found them on your own. And if such films spoke to you, discovering *Fangoria* was a revelation, because it showed you: a) that you were not alone; and b) that these films were quite often the work of very normal-looking individuals whose creativity was being channelled into this borderline disreputable material. As the decade progressed, *Fango* became that brand you trusted to point you toward your next horror fix.

EF: For 40 years, *Fangoria* has sat at the centre of a distinct subculture of horror fandom (also represented by festivals, conventions, and so on). For what reasons do you think horror has generated a more active fan-base than other genres?

PNJ: Horror fans see themselves as outsiders. With eleven seasons of *The Walking Dead*, and the rise of "elevated" horror, there's an argument that the "outsider" status is somewhat vestigial, but for decades horror fans have had a bit of a chip on their shoulder, and the pursuit of something perceived as "taboo" in their youth has required a certain amount of tenacity and passion. Some folks evolved past that sort of youthful rebellious banner waving about horror and found deeper rewards in the genre, but some still have the youthful excitement. But both factions are carrying out life sentences as horror fans. It doesn't go away.

EF: Arguably, this subculture has been sustained by its opposition to taste hierarchies — in other words, horror fans were redefining what could be called good art, championing films that were being overlooked or derided for being bad or offensive. To what extent has *Fangoria*, do you feel, supported independent or overlooked productions beside studio fare, and do you think it is democratic in its representation of the horror market?

PNJ: *Fango* presented Super-8 opuses alongside studio blockbusters, and the reader decided which title was worth their time. So it was a bit of a levelling force, and those low budget endeavours often became bigger cult classics than the studio stuff featured alongside them on the page. The big mark *Fango* left on the market was that it made horror cool. The FX artists featured in the mag looked like rock stars, and in some cases, the guys making these amazing FX were maybe six years older than us readers. They were big brothers we looked up to.

EF: Obviously fandoms are fluid things. How do you think horror fandom has changed over the years and to what end?

PNJ: I've seen horror fandom go from this outsider, secret handshake, loose affiliation to a cultural (and marketing) juggernaut, where people form their whole identities around horror culture. Romero, Hooper, Carpenter were all Cold War kids whose nightmare fuel was very real, existential concerns – and today a lot of horror is coming from people who only ever cared about horror films. I think it's debatable how healthy that's been for the genre – to me the most interesting horror is happening outside the *ouroboros*, with folks like Jordan Peele and Ari Aster taking big swings – but fandom has never been more self-assured and catered to than it is right now.

EF: Often the 1960s-1970s is seen to be horror's "golden age" (that is, the period Robin Wood brought to critical attention), but *Fangoria* came right at the end of

that period (1979-). Why do you think 1980s horror might have been neglected by scholarship, and why do you think it has developed such a different reputation?

PNJ: I think it's a "whores and old buildings" kind of mindset – generally, we need a couple of decades to look back at any particular movement with context and clarity (or, maybe more cynically, to deem it worthy of critical consideration). I think around 20 years after the 80s you started to see critical evaluations of that period, feminist and queer readings of slasher films, etc. So in many ways, the '80s has been getting its due in recent years. At the same time there's a lot of empty nostalgia for the '80s by folks who weren't there the first time, so re-evaluating the decade becomes, culturally, a bit of a mixed bag. That said, I do recall *Re-Animator* being rather well-received in the moment, and its humour and relative sophistication were, to me, always right there on the surface.

EF: What role do you think 'classic' horror films (including but not limited to *Re-Animator*) have to play within horror circles presently?

PNJ: I think horror fandom has a canon, and that canon is fairly democratic. We decide what films get to stay. We don't need an Academy, or a Hall of Fame. Every film in this "horror canon" is there because it deserves to be. Empire Pictures put out a LOT of movies, but *Re-Animator* is still talked about and still revered because of its quality, and there was nothing like it before (or since, really).

Bibliography

Abbott, S. (2010) "High Concept Thrills and Chills" in Conrich, I. (ed.) *Horror Zone*. London and New York: I.B. Tauris, pp. 27-44.

Aldana Reyes, X. (2014) *Body Gothic: Corporeal Transgression in Contemporary Literature and Horror Film*. University of Wales Press.

Arzen, M. (2004) "'There Is Only One': The Restoration of the Repressed in *The Exorcist: The Version You've Never Seen!*" in Hantke, S. (ed.) *Horror Film: Creating and Marketing Fear*. Mississippi: University Press of Mississippi, pp. 99-116.

Attanasio, P. (1985) "Captivating Cutups" (25th October). *The Washington Post*.

Badley, L. (2004) "The Darker Side of Genius: The (Horror) Auteur Meets Freud's Theory" in Schneider, S. J., (ed.) *Horror Film and Psychoanalysis: Freud's Worst Nightmare*. Cambridge: Cambridge University Press, pp. 222–240.

----- (2010) "Bringing It All Back Home: Horror Cinema and Video Culture" in Conrich, I., (ed.) *Horror Zone*. London and New York: I.B. Tauris, pp. 45-66.

Beauchamp, Z. (2018) "Incel, the misogynist ideology that inspired the deadly Toronto attack, explained" (25th April). *Vox*. Available at: https://www.vox.com/world/2018/4/25/17277496/incel-toronto-attack-alek-minassian (accessed March 2019).

Berenstein, R. (1996) *Attack of the Leading Ladies: Gender, Sexuality, and Spectatorship in Classic Horror Cinema*. New York: Columbia University Press.

Bernard, M. (2014) *Selling the Splat Pack: The DVD Revolution and the American Horror Film*. Edinburgh: Edinburgh University Press.

Blake, L. (2008) *The Wounds of Nations: Horror Cinema, Historical Trauma, and National Identity*. Manchester: New York: Manchester University Press.

Bordwell, D. (2007) *Poetics of Cinema*. New York: Routledge.

Botting, F. (1998) "Monstrosity" in Mulvey-Roberts, M. (ed.) *The Handbook to Gothic Literature*. New York: New York University Press, pp. 163-4.

BoxOfficeMojo, "1982 Domestic Grosses". *BoxOfficeMojo*. Available at: https://www.boxofficemojo.com/yearly/chart/?yr=1982&p=.htm (accessed March 2020).

Briefel, A. (2005) "Monster Pains: Masochism, Menstruation, and Identification in the Horror Film" in *Film Quarterly*, vol. 58, No. 3 (Spring), pp. 16-27.

Brody, M. (1987) "We Killed 'Em in Chicago" (February). *Film Comment*.

Brophy, P. (1986) "Horrality— The Textuality of Contemporary Horror Films" in *Screen*, Volume 27, Issue 1 (January/February), pp. 2–13.

Bundel, A. (2019) "'Joker,' starring Joaquin Phoenix, sparked an incel controversy because it's hopelessly hollow" (5th October). *NBC News*. Available at: https://www.nbcnews.com/think/opinion/joker-starring-joaquin-phoenix-sparked-incel-controversy-because-it-s-ncna1062656 (accessed March 2020).

Carlyle, T. (2007) "Sign of the Times" (1829) in Himmelfarb, G., (ed.) *The Spirit of the Age*. Yale University Press, pp. 31-49.

Carroll, N. (1999) "Horror and Humor." *The Journal of Aesthetics and Art Criticism*, vol. 57, no. 2. 145-160.

----- (2002) "Why Horror?" in Jancovich, M., (ed.) *Horror: The Film Reader*. New York: Routledge [1990]. Pp. 33-46.

Clayton, W. (2015) "Introduction" in Clayton, W., (ed.) *Style and Form in the Hollywood Slasher*. Basingstoke: Palgrave Macmillan. Pp. 1-14.

----- (2015) "Undermining the Moneygrubbers, or: How I Learned to Stop Worrying and Love *Friday the 13th Part V*" in Clayton, W. (ed.) *Style and Form in the Hollywood Slasher*. Basingstoke: Palgrave Macmillan, pp. 37-50.

----- (2020) *SEE! HEAR! CUT! KILL!: Experiencing Friday the 13th*. Jackson: University of Mississippi Press.

Clover, C. (1992) *Men, Women, and Chainsaws: Gender in the Modern Horror Film*. New Jersey: Princeton University Press.

Crampton, B. (2016) "Don't Call Me a Scream Queen" (16th December). *Birth-Movies-Death*. Available at: https://birthmoviesdeath.com/2016/12/15/barbara-crampton-dont-call-me-a-scream-queen (accessed September 2019).

Creed, B., (1993) "Dark Desires: Male Machoism in the Horror Film" in Cohan, S., Hark, I. R. (eds) *Screening the Male: Exploring Masculinities in Hollywood Cinema*. New York: Routledge, pp. 118-133.

----- (1993) *The Monstrous-Feminine: Film, Feminism, Psychoanalysis*. London and New York: Routledge.

Cubitt, S. (2009) "The Supernatural in Neo-Baroque Hollywood" in Buckland, W. (ed.) *Film Theory and Contemporary Hollywood Movies*. New York and London: Routledge, pp. 47-65.

Doherty, T. (1996) "Genre, Gender. And the *Aliens* Trilogy" in Grant, B. K. (ed.) *The Dread of Difference: Gender and the Horror Film*. Austin: University of Texas Press, pp. 181-199.

Ebert, R. (1985) "Re-Animator" (18th October). *RogerEbert.com*. Available at: https://www.rogerebert.com/reviews/re-animator-1985 (accessed November 2019).

Egan, K. (2007) *Trash or Treasure? Censorship and the Changing Meanings of the Video Nasties*. Manchester: Manchester University Press.

----- (2013) "A *Real* Horror Star: Articulating the Extreme Authenticity of Ingrid Pitt" in Egan, K., Thomas, S. (eds) *Cult Film Stardom: Offbeat Attractions and Processes of Cultification*. Basingstoke: Palgrave Macmillan, pp. 212-25.

EW Staff. (2008) "The Cult 25: The Essential Left-Field Movie Hits Since '83" (27th August). *Entertainment Weekly*. Available at: https://ew.com/gallery/cult-25-essential-left-field-movie-hits-83/?slide=314045#314045 (accessed November 2019).

Fallows, T. (2018) "'More than Rutting Bodies': Cambist Films, Quality Independents, and the 'Lost' Films of George A. Romero" in *Journal of Popular Film and Television*, 46:2. 82-94.

Falvey, E. (2019) "'I'll eat you up I love you so': Adaptation, Authorship, and Intermediality' in Spike Jonze's Where the Wild Things Are' in Moss-Wellington, W., Wilkins, K. (eds) *The Films of Spike Jonze*. Edinburgh: University of Edinburgh Press, pp. 33-45.

----- (2020) "Revisiting the Female Monster: Sex and Monstrosity in Contemporary Body Horror" in in Falvey, E., Hickinbottom, J., Wroot, J. (eds) *New Blood: Critical Approaches to Contemporary Horror*. Cardiff: University of Wales Press, pp. 203-24.

Fisher, D. (1985) "A Moist Zombie Movie" in *Fangoria*, 46, pp. 43-6.

Follows, S. (2017) *The Horror Report*. Self-published. Available at: https://stephenfollows.com/horrorreport/ (accessed January 2020).

Freud, S. (2003) *The Uncanny* [1919]. London: Penguin Books.

Frey, M. (2016) *Extreme Cinema: The Transgressive Rhetoric of Today's Art Film Culture*. New Brunswick, NJ: Rutgers University Press.

Gallagher, J. A. (1989) *Film Directors on Directing*. Westport: Greenwood Publishing Group.

Gelder, K. (2000) "Introduction to Part Three" in Gelder, K. (ed.) *The Horror Reader*. New York: Routledge, pp. 81-3.

Gonce, J. W. (1998) "Unspeakable Cuts: The Necronomicon on Film" in Harms, D., Gonce, J. W. (eds) *The Necronomicon Files: The Truth Behind Lovecraft's Legend*, pp. 225-80.

Gordon, J. (2018) "Let Guillermo del Toro Finally Make 'At the Mountains of Madness'" (5th March). *The Outline*. Available at: https://theoutline.com/post/3598/guillermo-del-toro-at-the-mountains-of-madness-revival?zd=2&zi=hlmcmxey (access December 2019).

Green, M. (2013) "A Darker Magic: Heterocosms and Bricolage in Moore's Recent Reworkings of Lovecraft" in Green, M. (ed.) *Alan Moore and the Gothic Tradition*. Manchester: Manchester University Press, pp. 253-75.

Grønstad, A. (2008) *Transfigurations: Violence, Death, and Masculinity in American Cinema*. Amsterdam: Amsterdam University Press.

Gross, E. (1990) "The Body of Signification" In Fletcher J., Benjamin, A. (eds) *Abjection, Melancholia, and Love: The Work of Julia Kristeva*. New York: Routledge, pp. 80-103.

Grossman, B. W. (2017) "The Lion King: A 'Blockbuster Feline' on Broadway and Beyond" in Rodothenous, G. (ed.) *The Disney Musical on Stage and Screen: Critical Approaches from Snow White to Frozen*. London: Bloomsbury, pp. 117-32.

Hantke, S. (2013) "From the Library of America to the Mountains of Madness: Recent Discourse on H. P. Lovecraft" in Simmons, D. (ed.), *New Critical Essay on H. P. Lovecraft*. New York: Palgrave Macmillan, pp. 135-56.

Hickinbottom, J. (2020) "A Master of Horror? The Making and Marketing of Takashi Miike's Horror Reputation" in Falvey, E., Hickinbottom, J., Wroot, J. (eds) *New Blood: Critical Approaches to Contemporary Horror*. Cardiff: University of Wales Press, pp. 83-105.

Hollows, J. (2003) "The Masculinity of Cult," in Jancovich, M., et al. (eds), *Defining Cult Movies: The Cultural Politics of Oppositional Taste*. Manchester: Manchester University Press, pp. 35–53.

Horeck, T., and T. Kendall (2011) (eds) *The New Extremism in Cinema: From France to Europe*. Edinburgh: Edinburgh University Press.

Hunter, I.Q. (2016) *Cult Film as a Guide to Life: Fandom, Adaptation and Identity*. London: Bloomsbury.

Hutcheon, L. (2006) *A Theory of Adaptation*. New York: Routledge.

Jay, D., T. Dewi and N. Shumate (2013) *Empire of the 'B's: The Mad Movie World of Charles Band*. Bristol: Hemlock Books.

Jess-Cooke, C. (2009) *Film Sequels: Theory and Practice from Hollywood to Bollywood*. Edinburgh: University of Edinburgh Press.

Jones, M. (2013) "Tentacles and Teeth: The Lovecraftian Being in Popular Culture", in Simmons, D. (ed.) *New Critical Essays on H. P. Lovecraft*. New York: Palgrave Macmillan, pp. 227-48.

Jones, S. (2013) *Torture Porn: Popular Horror After Saw*. Basingstoke: Palgrave Macmillan.

Joshi, S.T. (1996) *H.P. Lovecraft: A Life*. United States: Necronomicon Press.

----- (2011) "Introduction" in Lovecraft, H. P., *The Call of Cthulhu and Other Weird Stories*. London: Penguin Books, pp. ix-xxvii.

----- (2013) "Foreward" in Simmons, D. (ed.) *New Critical Essays on H.P. Lovecraft*. New York: Palgrave Macmillan, pp. xi-xvi.

Joshi, S.T. and D. Schultz, (2005) *H. P. Lovecraft: Letters to Rheinhart Kleiner*. New York: Hippocampus Press.

Kael, P. (1990) *Hooked: Film Writings, 1985-88*. United Kingdom: Marion Boyars Publishers Ltd.

Kawin, B. (2012) *Horror and the Horror Film*. Wimbledon: Anthem Press.

Kehr, D. (1985) "Re-Animator: Review". *Chicago Reader*. Available at: https://www.chicagoreader.com/chicago/re-animator/Film?oid=1060504 (accessed Septem-ber 2019).

Kendrick, J. (2016) "Slasher Films and Gore in the 1980s" in Benshoff, H. M. (ed.) *A Companion to the Horror Film*. Chichester: Wiley-Blackwell, pp. 310-328.

Klinger, B. (2006) *Beyond the Multiplex: Cinema, New Technologies, and the Home*. Berkeley: University of California Press.

Kristeva J. (1982) *Powers of Horror: An Essay on Abjection*. New York: Columbia University Press.

Leeder, M. (2019) "The Limits of Knowledge: David Robert Mitchell's It Follows" in Bacon, S. (ed.) *Horror: A Companion*. Oxford, New York: Peter Lang, pp. 11-18.

Lester, C. (2021) *Horror Films for Children: Fear and Pleasure in American Cinema*. New York and London: Bloomsbury.

Lévy, M. (1988) *Lovecraft: A Study in the Fantastic*, trans. Joshi, S. T. Detroit: Wayne State University Press.

Lewis, J. (2007) *American Film: A History*. New York: W. W. Norton & Company.

Lovecraft, H. P. and S. T. Joshi, (2011) *The Call of Cthulhu and Other Weird Stories*. London: Penguin Books.

Maltby, R. (1998) "'Nobody Knows Everything': Post-Classical Historiography and Consolidated Entertainment' in Neale, S., Smith, M., *Contemporary Hollywood Cinema*. London: New York: Routledge, pp. 21-44.

Marlin, J. (1985) "Screen: Stuart Gordon Directs Re-Animator" (18th October). *New York Times*. Available at: https://www.nytimes.com/1985/10/18/movies/screen-stuart-gordon-directs-re-animator.html (accessed September 2019).

Mathijs, E. (2010) "They're Here! Special Effects in the Horror Cinema of the 1970s and 1980s" in Conrich, I. (ed.) *Horror Zone: The Cultural Experience of Contemporary Horror Cinema*. London and New York: I.B. Tauris, pp. 153-172.

Mathijs, E., and X. Mendik. (2008) "What is cult film?" in Mathijs, E., Mendik, X. (eds) *The Cult Film Reader*. New York: Open University Press, pp. 1-13.

Mathijs, E. and J. Sexton, (2011a) *100 Cult Films*. London: BFI Publishing.

----- (2011b) *Cult Cinema: An Introduction*. Chichester: Wiley-Blackwell.

McDonald, P. (2008) in Wasko, J. *The Contemporary Hollywood Film Industry*. Chichester: Wiley-Blackwell.

McGee, M. (1987) "The Band Plays on" in *Fangoria*, 68, pp. 54-7.

McKenna, M. (2017) "Whose Canon is it Anyway? Subcultural Capital, Cultural Distinction and Value in High Art and Low Culture Film Distribution" in Wroot, J. and Willis, A. (eds) *Cult Media: Re-Packed, Re-Released and Restored*. Basingstoke: Palgrave Macmillan, pp. 31-48.

Mendik, X. (2020) "From Midnight Movies to Mainstream Excess: Cult Horror Festivals and the Academy" in Falvey, E., Hickinbottom, J., Wroot, J. (eds) *New Blood: Critical Approaches to Horror*. Cardiff: University of Wales Press, pp. 53-78.

Migliore, A. and J. Stryslik. (2006) *The Lurker in the Lobby: A Guide to the Cinema of H.P. Lovecraft*. San Francisco: Night Shade Books.

Nakahara, T. (2010) "Making Up Monsters: Set and Costume Design in Horror Films" in Conrich, I. (ed.) *Horror Zone: The Cultural Experience of Contemporary Horror Cinema*. London and New York: I.B. Tauris, pp. 139-52.

Ndalianis, A. (2004) *Neo-Baroque Aesthetics and Contemporary Entertainment*. Cambridge, Massachusetts: The MIT Press.

Newman, K., "Trancers review". *Empire Magazine*. Available at: https://www.empireonline.com/movies/trancers/review/ (accessed March 2019).

Nowell, R. (2011) *Blood Money: A History of the First Teen Slasher Film Cycle*. New York and London: Continuum.

----- (2014) (ed.) *Merchants of Menace: The Business of Horror Cinema*. New York and London: Bloomsbury.

O'Toole, L. (2008) "The Cult of Horror" [1979] in Mathijs, E., Mendik, X. (eds) *The Cult Film Reader*. New York: Open University Press, pp. 257-263.

Paul, W. (1994) *Laughing/Screaming: Modern Hollywood Horror and Comedy*. New York: Columbia University Press.

Pheasant-Kelly, F. (2015) "Reframing Parody and Intertextuality in *Scream*: Formal Approaches to the 'Postmodern' Slasher" in Clayton, W. (ed.) *Style and Form in the Hollywood Slasher*. Basingstoke: Palgrave Macmillan, pp. 149-60.

Pineda, I. C. (2004) "Postmodern Elements of the Contemporary Horror Film" in Prince, S. (ed.) *The Horror Film*. New Brunswick, New Jersey: Rutgers University Press, pp. 85-116.

Prince, S. (1999) *A New Pot of Gold: Hollywood Under the Electronic Rainbow*, 1980-89. Berkley: University of California Press.

Robinson, S. (2000) *Marked Men: White Masculinity in Crisis*. New York: Columbia University Press.

Rose, S. (2017) "How post-horror movies are taking over cinema" (6th July), *The Guardian*. Available at: https://www.theguardian.com/film/2017/jul/06/post-horror-films-scary-movies-ghost-story-it-comes-at-night (accessed 29 August 2019).

Rowles, D. (2010) "Percentage-Wise, The 20 Most Profitable Movies of All Time" (28th June), *Pajiba*. Available at: http://www.pajiba.com/seriously_random_lists/percentagewise-the-20-most-profitable-movies-of-all-time.php (accessed May 2019).

Sconce, J. (2010) "Trashing the Academy: Taste, Excess, and an Emerging Politics of Cinematic Style" in Conrich, I. (ed.) *Horror Zone: The Cultural Experience of Contemporary Horror Cinema*. London and New York: I.B. Tauris, pp. 103-122.

Schatz, T. (2008) "The Studio System and Contemporary Hollywood" in McDonald, P., Wasko, J., (eds) *The Contemporary Hollywood Film Industry*. Chichester: Wiley-Blackwell, pp. 13-42.

Schneider, S. J. (2009) *101 Horror Movies You Must See Before You Die*. London: Cassell Illustrated.

Shelley, M. (2003) *Frankenstein: Or, The Modern Prometheus* [1818]. London: Penguin Books.

Simmons, D. (2013) *New Critical Essays on H.P. Lovecraft*. New York: Palgrave Macmillan.

SlantMagazine, (2019) "The 100 Greatest Horror Films of All Time" (25th October). *SlantMagazine*. Available at: https://www.slantmagazine.com/film/the-100-greatest-horror-movies-of-all-time/ (accessed February 2019).

Smith, D. G. (2006) *H.P. Lovecraft in Popular Culture: The Works and Their Adaptations in Film, Television, Comics, Music and Games*. North Carolina: MacFarland & Co.

Staiger, J. (2013) "Independent of What? Sorting Out Differences From Hollywood" in Geoff King, Claire Molloy, Yannis Tzioumakis (eds) *American Independent Cinema: Indie, Indiewood and Beyond*. New York: Routledge, pp. 15-27.

Stam, R. (2000) "Beyond Fidelity: The Dialogics of Adaptation", in Naremore, J. (ed.) *Film Adaptation*. New Jersey: Rutgers University Press, pp. 54-76.

Steven, M. (2017) *Splatter Capital: A Guide for Surviving the Horror Movie We Collectively Inhabit*. London: Repeater Books.

Thomas, K. (1985) "MOVIE REVIEW: 'RE-ANIMATOR' COULD BECOME A CLASSIC" (25th October). *Los Angeles Times*. Available at: https://www.latimes.com/archives/la-xpm-1985-10-25-ca-14442-story.html (accessed September 2019).

Thomas, S. (2013) "'Marginal moments of spectacle': Character Actors, Cult Stardom and Hollywood Cinema" in Egan, K., Thomas, S. (eds.) *Cult Film Stardom: Offbeat Attractions and Processes of Cultification*. Basingstoke: Palgrave Macmillan, pp. 37-56.

Tompkins, J. (2014) 'Bids for Distinction: The Critical-Industrial Function of the Horror Auteur" in Nowell, R. (ed.) *Merchants of Menace: The Business of Horror Cinema*. London: Bloomsbury, pp. 203-214.

Tudor, A. (1991) *Monsters and Mad Scientists: A Cultural History of the Horror Movie*. Chichester: Wiley-Blackwell.

----- (2002) "From Paranoia to Postmodernism? The Horror Movie in Late Modern Society" in Neale, S (ed.) *Genre and Contemporary Hollywood*. London: BFI, pp. 105-16.

Tzioumakis, Y. (2017) *American Independent Cinema: Second Edition*. Edinburgh: Edinburgh University Press.

Verini, B. (2011) "Re-Animator: The Musical" review (9th March). *Variety*. Available at: https://variety.com/2011/film/reviews/re-animator-the-musical-1117944790/ (accessed February 2019).

Walker, J. (2015) *Contemporary British Horror Cinema: Industry, Genre and Society*. Edinburgh: Edinburgh University Press.

Wasser, F. (2001) *Veni, Vidi, Video: The Hollywood Empire and the VCR*. Austin: University of Texas Press.

Wiator, S. (1992) "Interview with Stuart Gordon" in *Dark Visions*. New York: Avon.

Worland, R. (2006) *The Horror Film: An Introduction*. New Jersey: Wiley-Blackwell.

Wood, R. (2001) "The American Nightmare: Horror in the 70s" [1979] in Jancovich, M (ed.) *Horror, the Film Reader*. New York: Routledge, pp. 25-33.

----- (1986) *Hollywood From Vietnam to Reagan*. New York: Columbia University Press.

Woolford, J. (2017) "Where Did We Go Right (And Wrong)? Success and Failure in the Adaptations of The Producers from and to the Screen" in Rodothenous, G. (ed.) *Twenty-First Century Musicals: From Stage to Screen*. London: Routledge, pp. 80-93.

Wroot, J. (2020) "Bloody Muscles on VHS: When Asia Extreme Met the Video Nasties" in Falvey, E., Hickinbottom, J., Wroot, J. (eds) *New Blood: Critical Approaches to Horror*. Cardiff: University of Wales Press, pp. 107-23.

Wroot, J. and A. Willis. (2017) *Cult Media: Re-Packed, Re-Released and Restored*. Basingstoke: Palgrave Macmillan.

Wyatt, J. (1994) *High Concept: Movies and Marketing in Hollywood*. Austin: University of Texas Press.

Zinoman, J. (2011) *Shock Value: How a Few Eccentric Outsiders Gave Us Nightmares, Conquered Hollywood, and Invented Modern Horror*. London: Duckworth Overlook.

Žižek, S. (2001) *Enjoy Your Symptom! Jacques Lacan in Hollywood and Out*. New York: Routledge.

Zoglin, R. (1984) "Show Business: Gremlins in the Rating System" (25th June). *Time*. Available at: http://content.time.com/time/magazine/article/0,9171,926639,00.html (accessed March 2019).

Selected Filmography

2001: A Space Odyssey. 1968, USA, dir. Stanley Kubrick.

Alchemist, The. 1983, USA, dir. James Amante (Charles Band).

Alien. 1979, USA, dir. Ridley Scott.

Aliens. 1986, USA, dir. James Cameron.

American Beauty. 1999, USA, dir. Sam Mendes.

American Werewolf in London, An. 1981, USA/UK, dir. John Landis.

Animal House. 1978, USA, dir. John Landis.

Amityville Horror, The. 1979, USA, dir. Stuart Rosenberg.

Arena. 1989, USA, dir. Peter Manoogian.

Bad Taste. 1987, New Zealand, dir. Peter Jackson.

Barbarella. 1968, USA, dir. Roger Vadim.

Beyond Re-Animator. 2003, Spain/USA, dir. Brian Yuzna.

Black Cat, The from *Masters of Horror*, season 2, episode 11. 2007, USA, dir. Stuart Gordon.

Blade Runner. 1982, USA, dir. Ridley Scott.

Blair Witch Project, The. 1999, USA, dirs. Daniel Myrick and Eduardo Sánchez.

Bride of Re-Animator. 1990, USA, dir. Brian Yuzna.

Cabin in the Woods, The. 2012, USA, dir. Drew Goddard.

Candyman. 1992, USA, dir. Bernard Rose.

Cannibal Holocaust. 1980, Italy, dir. Ruggero Deodato.

Carrie. 1976, USA, dir. Brian De Palma.

Color Out of Space. 2019, USA, dir. Richard Stanley.

Creepshow. 1982, USA, dir. George A. Romero.

Dagon. 2001, USA, dir. Stuart Gordon.

Dentist, The. 1996, USA, dir. Brian Yuzna.

Dolls. 1987, USA, dir. Stuart Gordon.

Dorm that Dripped Blood, The. 1982, USA.

Dreams in the Witch House from *Masters of Horror*, season 1, episode 2. 2006, USA, dir. Stuart Gordon.

Evil Dead, The. 1981, USA, dir. Sam Raimi.

Evil Dead II. 1987, USA, dir. Sam Raimi.

Exorcist, The. 1973, USA, dir. William Friedkin.

Fly, The. 1986, USA, dir. David Cronenberg.

Frankenstein. 1931, USA, dir. James Whale.

Friday the 13th. 1980, USA, dir. Sean S. Cunningham.

From Beyond. 1986, USA, dir. Stuart Gordon.

Ghostbusters. 1984, USA, dir. Ivan Reitman.

Ghoulies. 1985, USA, dir. Luca Bercovici.

Gremlins. 1984, USA, dir. Joe Dante.

Halloween. 1978, USA, dir. John Carpenter.

House on Haunted Hill. 1999, USA, dir. William Malone.

It Follows. 2014, USA, dir. David Robert Mitchell.

Jaws. 1975, USA, dir. Steven Spielberg.

Lovecraft Country. 2020—, USA, HBO.

Lurking Fear, The. 1994, USA, dir. C. Courney Joyner.

Nightmare on Elm Street, A. 1984, USA, dir. Wes Craven.

Night of the Living Dead. 1968, USA, dir. George A. Romero.

Pit and the Pendulum, The. 1991, USA, dir. Stuart Gordon.

Poltergeist. 1982, USA, dir. Tobe Hooper.

Prince of Darkness. 1987, USA, dir. John Carpenter.

Re-Animator. 1985, USA, dir. Stuart Gordon.

Re-Penetrator. 2004, USA, dir. The Evil Carrot.

Return of the Living Dead. 1985, USA, dir. Dan O'Bannon.

Return of the Living Dead III. 1993, USA, dir. Brian Yuzna.

Robot Jox. 1989, USA, dir. Stuart Gordon.

Rocky Horror Picture Show, The. 1975, USA, dir. Jim Sharman.

Savage Island. 1985, USA, dir. Nicholas Beardsley.

Saw. 2004, USA, dir. James Wan.

Scream. 1996, USA, dir. Wes Craven.

Shining, The. 1980, USA, dir. Stanley Kubrick.

Society. 1989, USA, dir. Brian Yuzna.

Superman. 1978, USA, dir. Richard Donner.

Texas Chainsaw Massacre, The. 1974, USA, dir. Tobe Hooper.

They Live. 1988, USA, dir. John Carpenter.

Thing, The. 1982, USA, dir. John Carpenter.

Trancers. 1984, USA, dir. Charles Band.

Walking the Edge. 1985, USA, dir. Norbert Meisel.

Young Frankenstein. 1974, USA, dir. Mel Brooks.

Devil's Advocates

"Auteur Publishing's new Devil's Advocates critiques on individual titles offer bracingly fresh perspectives from passionate writers. The series will perfectly complement the BFI archive volumes." Christopher Fowler, Independent on Sunday

Creepshow – Simon Brown

Released in cinemas in 1982, Creepshow is typically regarded as a minor entry in both the film output of George A. Romero and the history of adaptations of the works of Stephen King. It is here reassessed by Simon Brown, who examines the making and release of the film and its legacy through a comic book adaptation and two sequels.

The Evil Dead – Lloyd Haynes

This lively account of the making and reception of one of the most inventive and energetic of all horror movies also considers how it creates its 'bad dream' effect, the importance of its 'bad place' motif, male hero Ash's similarities to the 'Final Girl' trope, and the film's notorious reputation in Britain as a 'video nasty'.

Shivers – Luke Aspell

Shivers (1975) was David Cronenberg's first commercial feature and his first horror film. Luke Aspell's analysis addresses all aspects of its production, including shot composition, lighting, cinematographic texture, sound, the use of stock music, editing, costume, makeup, optical work, the screenplay, the casting, and the direction of the actors.

www.ingramcontent.com/pod-product-compliance
Lightning Source LLC
Chambersburg PA
CBHW051543230426
43669CB00015B/2711